Written That You May Believe

Written That You May Believe

21 Ruminations on the Gospel of John

RODNEY BOYD

WordCrafts

Written That You May Believe
Copyright © 2018
Rodney Lewis Boyd

Cover concept and design by David Warren.

All rights reserved. No part of this book may be reproduced, stored in a retrieval system, or transmitted in any form or by any means—electronic, mechanical, photocopy, recording or otherwise—without the prior written permission of the publisher. The only exception is brief quotations for review purposes.

Unless otherwise noted, all scripture quotations are taken from the New American Standard Bible®, Copyright © 1960, 1962, 1963, 1968, 1971, 1972, 1973, 1975, 1977, 1995 by The Lockman Foundation. Used by permission. (www.Lockman.org)

Scripture quotations marked "AMP" taken from the Amplified® Bible, Copyright © 1954, 1958, 1962, 1964, 1965, 1987 by The Lockman Foundation Used by permission. (www.Lockman.org)

Scripture quotations marked "KJV" taken from the King James Version of the Bible, public domain.

All references to "Strong's" refer to Strong's Exhaustive Concordance of the Bible, public domain.

Published by WordCrafts Press
Cody, Wyoming 82414
www.wordcrafts.net

I dedicate this book about believing to the one who led me to the Lord as she showed me why to believe:

To Brenda,
my fellow traveler and fellow believer since 1970.

Contents

INTRODUCTION 1
IN THE BEGINNING 5
THE BEST FOR NOW 12
YE MUST BE 23
THE COMING HOUR 33
WHO IS THE MAN? 41
FULL OF WONDERFUL BREAD 46
FLOWING RIVERS 53
FREE INDEED 57
DISPLAYED WORKS 63
ABUNDANT LIFE 72
LAZARUS UNWRAPPERS 78
DEATH OF A GRAIN 83
THE EXAMPLE 87
ANOTHER HELPER/COMFORTER 93
THE CONNECTION 98
DO YOU NOW BELIEVE 102
TRUTH 108
WHAT IS TRUTH 115
GIVEN AUTHORITY 120
LIFE IN HIS NAME 124
FOLLOW ME 132
WRITTEN THAT YOU MAY BELIEVE OVERVIEW 137
ABOUT THE AUTHOR 141

INTRODUCTION

The Gospel of John is one of the 66 books in the library called the Holy Bible. It is one of the four books entitled he Gospels. There is the Gospel According to Matthew, Mark, Luke, and John. Each one of these Gospels is written from a perspective directed to various audiences. When you read them together, you have an overview of an eyewitness account about Jesus the Christ.

The first three Gospels are known as "synoptic" Gospels. According to Dictionary.com synoptic is defined as, "taking a common view: used chiefly in reference to the first three Gospels (synoptic Gospels) Matthew, Mark, and Luke, from their similarity in content, order, and statement."

The Gospel of John is known as the "discourse" Gospel. A discourse is defined in Dictionary.com as, "communication of thought by words; talk; conversation: earnest and intelligent discourse and a formal discussion of a subject in speech or writing, as a dissertation, treatise, sermon."

The common thread found throughout all four Gospels is

Jesus the Christ, Who was born, lived and died, and was resurrected. The synoptic Gospels have stories, parables, sayings, and sermons that focus on Jesus and His purpose which was to, "destroy the works of the d-evil." (1 John 3:8, addition mine) The Gospel of John is different from the other three Gospels in that John presents multiple "discourses" that Jesus taught.

NOTE: Throughout this book you will see name of the devil with a hyphen between the /d/ and the /e/. This shows the d-evil is the evil one. Also, I refuse to show the d-evil any respect by capitalizing his name.

Each Gospel is written for specific audiences and purposes under the anointing of the Holy Ghost.

- Matthew: Written to a Jewish audience
- Mark: Written to a Roman audience
- Luke: Written to a Gentile audience
- John: Written to whosoever (a general audience)

As we focus on the Gospel according to John, we see why this Gospel was written.

> *"Many other signs (attesting miracles) therefore Jesus also performed in the presence of the disciples, which are not written in this book; but these things have been written that you may believe that Jesus is the Christ, the Son of God; and that believing you may have life in His name."*
> (John 20:30-31, emphasis mine)

Yes, there is an agenda in the writing of this Gospel. The agenda is rooted in believing about specific things.

INTRODUCTION

"The word 'believe' (trust, adhere to, rely on) occurs ninety-eight times throughout this book. The assured result of this belief or faith in Jesus Christ is the possession of eternal life." (Introduction to the Gospel According to John in the Amplified Bible)"

BELIEVE: pisteuō (pist-yoo'-o)=From G4102; to have faith (in, upon, or with respect to, a person or thing), that is, credit; by implication to entrust (especially ones spiritual well- being to Christ): - believe (-r), commit (to trust), put in trust with. G4102: pistis (pis'-tis)=From G3982; persuasion, that is, credence; moral conviction (of religious truth, or the truthfulness of God or a religious teacher), especially reliance upon Christ for salvation; abstractly constancy in such profession; by extension the system of religious (Gospel) truth itself: - assurance, belief, believe, faith, fidelity. G3082: peithō (pi'-tho)=A primary verb; to convince (by argument, true or false); by analogy to pacify or conciliate (by other fair means); reflexively or passively to assent (to evidence or authority), to rely (by inward certainty): - agree, assure, believe, have confidence, be (wax) content, make friend, obey, persuade, trust, yield. (Strong's)

These things were written so that you may believe:

- That Jesus is the Christ.
- That Jesus is the Son of God.
- That by believing you may have life in His name.

If I were to recommend a book of the Bible to someone who was not a believer, I would recommend The Gospel according to John, so that they would have the opportunity to believe.

This book, *Written That You May Believe: 21 Ruminations from The Gospel of John,* was written as a book *about* a book. The expanse of the Gospel according to John prohibits our purposes a verse-by-verse study of the discourse. We will glean nuggets from John's writings and focus on specific topics.

There are 21 chapters in the Gospel according to John and there are 21 chapters in this book. I suggest that before you read each chapter of this book, that you read each corresponding chapter from the Gospel of John. At the end of each chapter in this book, there is a section called, "Written That You May Believe," where I make a brief declaration of belief. Feel free to write out and declare you own personal declaration of belief.

To effectively read, *Written That You May Believe: 21 Ruminations on The Gospel of John,* you will need a pencil/pen and a Bible of your choice. I personally use The New American Standard Bible, but also use other translations.

My prayer is that you will come out on the other side of this book believing.

Rodney Lewis Boyd

IN THE BEGINNING

"In the beginning was the Word, *and the* Word *was with God, and the* Word *was God. He was in the beginning with God."*

(John 1:1-2, emphasis mine)

John starts off Chapter One setting the tone for the whole book. What you believe about Jesus is the whole crux of the matter. Jesus is not just another man with a God complex. Jesus is not just a good man, or a great teacher, or a pious prophet. Jesus is God in the flesh.

Every cult, sect, and religion portray Christ as less than He is. They lower Him to the level of their gods, their prophets, and their teachers. For example, there is a cult that utilizes their own translation, with John 1:1 lowering Jesus to the level of being a god. Orthodox Christianity believes that Jesus was not a god (little g) but is God (big G).

"In the beginning was the Word, and the Word was with

God, and the Word was a god."
(John 1:1, NWT, emphasis mine)

Either this Word was God (Big G) or was a god (little g). We can effectively change Word and replace it with Jesus to get the full effect of Who Jesus is, God in the flesh.

"In the beginning was Jesus, *and* Jesus *was with God, and* Jesus *was God.* Jesus *was in the beginning with God. All things came into being through* Jesus; *and apart from* Jesus *nothing came into being that has come into being."*
(John 1:1, emphasis mine)

In the Epistle (a letter) to the Hebrews, the first thing underscored concerns the nature of Jesus. (By the way; an epistle is not the wife of an apostle. I will leave you a little time to chuckle at that joke.) Now; on with what the writer of the book of Hebrews—under the anointing of the Holy Spirit—says about Jesus.

"God (The Father), after He (God) spoke long ago to the fathers in the prophets in many portions and in many ways, in these last days has spoken to us in His Son (Jesus), Whom He (God the Father) appointed heir of all things, and through Whom also He (Jesus) made the world, and He (Jesus) is the radiance of His glory and the exact representation of His (God the Father) nature, and upholds all things by the word of His (Jesus) power. When He (Jesus) had made purification of sins, He (Jesus) sat down at the right hand of the Majesty (God the Father) on high; having become much more than the angels, as He (Jesus)

has inherited a more excellent name than they."
(Hebrews 1:1-4, addition mine)

The apostle Paul underscores what the writer of Hebrews tells us.

"For in Him (Jesus) all things were created, both in the heavens and on the earth, visible and invisible, whether thrones or dominions or rulers or authorities—all things have been created through Him (Jesus) and for Him (Jesus). And He (Jesus) is before all things, and in Him (Jesus) all things come together."
(Colossians 1:16-17, addition mine)

Now, that is pretty powerful stuff from "just a man."
As mentioned at the beginning of this chapter, one thing in common with various cults is the attack on the deity of Jesus, trying to bring Him down to the level of a mere mortal instead of God in the flesh. We see in the First Epistle of John that to deny that Jesus came in the flesh is rooted in the spirit of antichrist (anti/against-The Anointed One).

"Children, it is the last hour; and just as you heard that antichrist is coming, even now many antichrists have arisen; from this we know that it is the last hour."
(1 John 2:18)

The lie of the antichrist is denial. The denial is this:

"Who is the liar but the one who denies that Jesus is the Christ? This is the antichrist, the one who denies the Father

and the Son (Jesus)."

(1 John 2:22, addition mine)

The denial comes in the form of denying His anointing from the Father. Denial of the fact that God came to Earth in the form of a human being as a baby and grew up into a man Who was anointed by God with the Holy Spirit and Power. Denial of how He went about doing good and healing all who were oppressed by the d-evil for God was with Him (Immanuel = God with us). Then He (Jesus) went to the cross in our place to pay our debt, He died, and then on the third day He (Jesus) rose from the dead and then returned to heaven with a promise that He would return again. (See Matthew 1:20-25, Luke 1:26-38, Matthew 3:11-17, Matthew 4:23-24, Acts 10:38, Luke 24:49, Acts 1:4-11)

John tells us one of the reasons that he wrote 1 John was concerning the deceivers/antichrist.

"These things have I written to you concerning those who are trying to deceive you."

(1 John 2:26)

At the time of the writing of this epistle, there was a rise of a group of people within the church called the Gnostics (the G is silent). I like to call them the Nasty Gnostics. Here is a description of the heresy of Gnosticism found in the introduction of The First Letter (epistle) of John in the Ryrie Study Bible.

"The heresy of Gnosticism had begun to make inroads among churches in John's day. Among its teachings were:

- Knowledge is superior to virtue
- The nonliteral sense of Scripture is correct and can be understood only by a select few
- Evil in the world precludes God's being the only Creator
- The incarnation is incredible because deity cannot unite itself with anything material such as a body Docetism (an early Christian doctrine that the sufferings of Christ were apparent and not real and that after the crucifixion he appeared in a spiritual body; an ancient heresy asserting that Jesus lacked full humanity) Definition of Docetism is from Dictionary.com
- There is no resurrection of the flesh."

The ethical standards of many Gnostics were low, so John emphasized the reality of the Incarnation and the high ethical standard of the earthly life of Christ.

According to the Ryrie Study Bible, the crux of the matter is that, "the incarnation (the doctrine that the second person of the Trinity assumed human form in the person of Jesus Christ and is completely both God and man) is incredible because deity cannot unite itself with anything material." This is denying that Jesus came in the flesh.

> *"Beloved, do not believe every spirit, but test the spirit to see whether they are from God; because many false prophets have gone out into the world. By this you know the Spirit of God; every spirit that confess that Jesus Christ has come in the flesh is from God and every spirit that does not confess Jesus (has come in the flesh) is not from God; and this is the spirit of the antichrist, of which you have heart that it is*

coming, and no it is already in the world."

(1 John 4:1-3, addition mine)

JOHN 1:1-14 WORD/JESUS VERSION

With all this being said, let's read the Gospel of John, chapter one, verses one through fourteen. Everywhere it says, "the Word," or "He," or "Him," replace them with the name of Jesus.

"In the beginning was Jesus, and Jesus was with God, and Jesus was God. Jesus was in the beginning with God. All things came into being through Jesus; and apart from Jesus nothing came into being that has come into being. In Jesus was life; and the life was the light of men. And the light (of Jesus) shines in the darkness; and the darkness did not comprehend it. There came a man sent from God whose name was John. He came for a witness, that he might bear witness of the light (of Jesus), that all might believe through him. He was not the light (of Jesus), but came that he might bear witness of the light (of Jesus). There was the true light (Jesus) which, coming into the world enlightens every man. Jesus was in the world, and the world was made through Jesus, and the world did not know Jesus. Jesus came to His (Jesus) own and those who were His (Jesus) own did not receive Jesus. But as many as received Jesus, to them He (the Father) gave the right to become children of God, even to those who believe in Jesus' name who were born not of blood, nor the will of the flesh, nor of the will of man, but of God. And Jesus became flesh, and dwelt among us, and

we beheld Jesus' glory, glory as the only begotten from the Father, full of grace and truth."
(John 1:1-14, addition mine)

John wrote these things that you may believe that Jesus is God in the flesh. If this is a fact, then that underscores Who He should be to you. If you believe that Jesus is God in the flesh, this solidifies your belief the creation of the world. When you come into the knowledge of Jesus as God the Creator—and that creation is when The Word is expressed aloud—then you have crossed from darkness into the "let there be" light. How wonderful that we as human beings have beheld the glory as the only begotten from the Father.

WRITTEN THAT YOU MAY BELIEVE

Lord, I believe that You are the Word that became (God in the) flesh and dwelt among us.

2

THE BEST FOR NOW

"And He said to them, "Draw some out now and take it to the headwaiter." So they took it to him, and when the headwaiter tasted the water which had become wine, and did not know where it came from (but the servants who had drawn the water knew), the headwaiter called the bridegroom, and said to him, 'Everyman serves the good wine first, and when men have drunk freely (have become drunk), then that which is poorer; you have *kept the good wine until now.'"*

(John 2:8-10, emphasis mine)

"*Then He told them, 'Now draw some out and take it to the master of the banquet.' They did so, and the master of the banquet tasted the water that had been turned into wine. He did not realize where it had come from, though the servants who had drawn the water knew. Then he called the bridegroom aside and said, "Everyone brings out the choice wine first and then the cheaper wine after the guests have had too much to drink; but* you have saved the best till now."

(John 2:8-10, NIV, emphasis mine)

For thirty years, Jesus had grown physically into a man. He had entered the waters of the Jordan River by obedience to the Father, to be baptized by his cousin, John the Baptist. Now, John was not of the Baptist denomination, because at that time there were no denominations to muddy the waters so to speak. If he should be called anything it should be, John the Dipper.

BAPTIZE: baptizō (bap-tid'-zo)=From a derivative of G911; to make whelmed (that is, fully wet); used only (in the New Testament) of ceremonial ablution, especially (technically) of the ordinance of Christian baptism: - baptist, baptize, wash. G911: baptō (bap'-to)=A primary verb; to whelm, that is, cover wholly with a fluid; in the New Testament only in a qualified or specific sense, that is, (literally) to moisten (a part of one's person), or (by implication) to stain (as with dye): -DIP. (Strong's)

As Jesus stepped into the waters and was dipped fully immersed with the waters, He came up and the Holy Spirit, in the form of a dove, came upon Him and stayed. After Jesus fulfilled obedience to the Father, the Father affirmed His pleasure with His Son. (Matthew 3:1-17) Jesus was then tempted in the wilderness and came out the other side of the wilderness in, "the power of the Spirit..." (Matthew 4:1-11; Luke 4:14; John 1:25-34)

Jesus, under the anointing of the Holy Spirit and power (dynamic ability), was going about and doing good and healing all who were oppressed by the d-evil. He was teaching, proclaiming the gospel of the kingdom, and healing every kind of disease and sickness among the people including the ill, pains, demoniacs, epileptics, paralytics. He healed them all. (Matthew 4:23-24; Acts 10:38)

Before He started out for three years of manifesting God's Kingdom and God's will on Earth as it is in heaven, Jesus had to have a beginning of signs (attesting miracles which "points to the supernatural power of God in redeeming grace" margin notes in NASB). The beginning of signs and attesting miracles began at a social function called a wedding.

The wedding was not just a one-day ceremony but a one to two-week celebration. The origin of this coming together of a man and a woman is seen in the book of beginnings which is known as The Book of Genesis.

"In the beginning God..."

(Genesis 1:1)

CREATED: bârâ' (baw-raw')=A primitive root; (absolutely) to create; (qualified) to cut down (a wood), select, feed (as formative processes): - choose, create (creator), cut down, dispatch, do, make (fat). (Strong's)

Genesis starts with creation unfolding by the spoken Word as the Holy Spirit hovered over the chaotic, dark surface of the deep. The creative process in Genesis 1:1-25 included God:

- Said

- Saw
- Separated
- Called
- Made
- Placed
- Created
- Blessed

God's commentary on His creation was:

"God saw that it was good."

(Genesis 1:25)

After God created:

- The heavens and the earth
- Light and darkness separation
- Water and land
- Sprouting vegetation
- Plants yielding seed and fruit trees
- Evening and morning
- Two great lights: greater (for day) and lesser (for night)
- Waters teeming with swarms of living creatures
- Birds flying above the earth
- Great sea monsters
- Every living creature that moves which swarmed after their kind
- Every winged bird after its kind
- Living creatures of every kind including cattle, creeping things and beasts

As we have said, God saw and called it all His creations,

"*...good.*"

(Genesis 1:25)

God then came to the pinnacle of His creations, what some have called the "crown of creation:" Human beings. It appears that there is a discussion in the heavenly conference room with God and someone else that were involved in the creative process. I am thinking it was: (1) The Father, (2) The Son/Word, and (3) The Holy Spirit.

> "*Then God said,* 'Let Us *make man in* Our *image, according to* Our *likeness and let* them *rule over the fish of the sea and over the birds of the sky and over and over the cattle and over all the earth, and over every creeping thing that creeps on the earth.*' God *created man in his own image, in the image of God He created him;* male and female *He created them. God blessed* them; *and God said to* them, '*Be fruitful and multiply, and fill the earth, and subdue it; and rule over the fish of the sea and over the birds of the sky and over every living thing that moves on earth.*'"
>
> (Genesis 1:26-28, emphasis mine)

NOTE: Don't worry; we will be going back to the Gospel of John, but we are looking at the original marriage between a man and a woman and then see Jesus on the scene of a marriage.

As God created a man and woman and gave them both authority over all the created beings, we see a lot of genesis moments (aka beginnings):

- God creating man from a lump of clay.
- God breathing His breath into the nostrils of clay and jump starting the clay that became a living soul/being. This is the first CPR.
- God cause a deep sleep to fall upon man. This is the first anesthesia prior to surgery.
- God took a rib from the side of man. This is the first surgical procedure.
- God closed the flesh at place of *ribectomy*. This is the first surgical closure.
- God fashioned /formed the rib into a woman. This is the first fashion show.
- God brought the woman to the man. This is the first walk down the aisle bringing the bride to the man.
- The man said, "This is now bone of my bones, and flesh of my flesh; she shall be called Woman, because she was taken out of Man." This is the first self-written vows.
- The reason for the joining together of a man and a woman (aka marriage).

"For this reason a man shall leave his father and his mother and be joined to his wife; and they shall become one flesh, and the man and his wife were both naked and were not ashamed."

(Genesis 2:24)

In the Gospel of John, we see a wedding take place (the union of a man and woman) in Cana of Galilee. What took place in the Garden of Eden was now taking place as was the custom of marriage in Cana. The principals in this wedding included:

- Mary the mother of Jesus
- Jesus and His disciples (invited guest)
- Servants
- The headwaiter
- The bride
- The bridegroom
- People/guests (including Jesus and His disciples)

According to various resources (Commentary in Ryrie Study Bible, The Zondervan Handbook of the Bible, Eerdmans' Handbook of the Bible), the marriage ceremony was a week-long celebration custom that involved much merriment, including going to the home to get the betrothed bride and walking to the groom's home while singing and laughing. Once at the groom's home, food and drink flowed. It is at this point that our story begins.

We enter the story on day three in Cana of Galilee. Mary, the mother of Jesus, was there and it appears that she had something to do with the coordination of the celebration. Jesus and His disciples were present as invited guests. I cannot fathom Jesus just sitting around with no expression on his face, looking very pious and bringing everyone down. It may be my imagination, I can see Jesus entering into the joyous occasion, smiling, laughing, eating and drinking.

On day three, a problem occurred that was pointed out to Jesus. The wine ran out. Whenever there is a party at our house, the one thing that I am known for is that I cannot stand to not have enough food or drink. I would much rather have too much than too little.

When they ran out of wine, Mary turned to her Son Jesus to solve the problem.

> *"When the wine ran out, the mother of Jesus said to Him, 'They have no wine.'"*
>
> (John 2:3)

Jesus was an invited guest and not the supplier of the wine; however, there was no Cana Wines and Liquor Store to run to and replenish the stock. I have often wondered what Mary expected Jesus to do. Did she expect Him to turn water into wine?

Up to this point there were no attesting miracle done that would lead her to believe that He could as Larry Norman (Christian music artist) sang in the song "The Outlaw," talking about how Jesus would do tricks that would provide food and wine for weddings and other events.

Jesus responded to His mother with what some considered an insult and others considered a respectful response.

> *"And Jesus said to her, 'Woman, what does that have to do with us? My hour has not yet come.'"*
>
> (John 2:4)

It was at this point that we see the same attitude that Mary had at the announcement that she would be giving birth to the Messiah.

> *"And Mary said,' Behold the bond-slave of the Lord; may it be done to me according to your word…'"*
>
> (Luke 1:38)

Mary then spoke to the servants concerning the problem of no wine.

"His mother said to the servants, 'Whatever He says to you do it.'"

(John 2:5)

NOTE: I'm thinking that I need to practice the Mary attitude in my life,

"Lord, be it (whatever it is) according to your word,"

(Luke 1:38)

and

"whatever He says to you, do it."

(John 2:5).

Jesus took common objects that were used for the Jewish custom of purification; water pots. Isn't that how Jesus usually does a miracle, by taking common objects and using them to manifest His glory? These water pots would have contained twenty or thirty gallons (75-113 liters) of water. (That 75 to 113 liters would be a lot of soda pop.) God took a common lump of clay and breathe His breath and made it into a living being. (Genesis 2:7)

In Christ, a common man was made into a brand-new creation where the old things passed away. (2 Corinthians 5:17)

"Therefore, if anyone cleanses himself from these things, he will be a vessel for honor, sanctified, useful to the Master, prepared for every good work."

(2 Timothy 2:21)

Jesus told them to fill the water pots with water and draw some out and take it to the headwaiter, and then the servant did like Mary instructed, they did whatever Jesus said.

Now the plot thickens, as the headwaiter takes a drink of the water that had been turned into wine. From the point of the servants filling the pots with water to the point of when the headwaiter tasted the liquid, something took place. What happened was that the water had become wine. That something is called an, "attesting miracle." The headwaiter did not know where the wine came from (because they had run out of wine) but the servant who had drawn the water knew. The headwaiter called the bridegroom thinking the bridegroom had kept back the best wine.

> "...*the headwaiter called the bridegroom and said to him, 'Everyman serves the good wine first and when the people have drunk (and became drunk) freely, then he serves the poorer wine; but (in contrast to that)* you have kept the good (best) wine until now.'"
>
> (John 2:9-10, emphasis mine)

That is how our God is when He moves in our lives, He saves the best for now. As we live out our lives in the present time—the now—we can expect the best from God. His best comes from the common things in our lives.

In Cana, at a wedding, Jesus did the miraculous with miracles or attesting miracles. He demonstrated how He saved the best for now. He manifested His glory and, as a result, His disciples who followed Him by faith and His followers became more than just hopeful followers; they believed in Him.

"This beginning of his signs Jesus did in Cana of Galilee, and manifested His glory, and His disciples believed in Him."

(John 2:11)

NOTE: Some would say that miracles do not help anyone believe; but apparently Jesus' followers went from not believing to believing after seeing the attesting miracle.

Are you just a follower or are you a believer?

WRITTEN THAT YOU MAY BELIEVE

Lord, I believe that, like the wine that was the best for now, You are the best for me now.

3

YE MUST BE

"Marvel not that I said unto thee, 'Ye must be born again.'"
(John 3:7, KJV)

This is the story of a man named Nicodemus (Nick). He was religious man, a member of the Pharisees and, as a ruler of the Jews, had authority.

> *"Nicodemus, a ruler of the Jews, was a member of the Sanhedrin. He perfectly represents the aristocratic, well-intentioned but unenlightened Judaism of his day."*
> (Ryrie Study Bible note on John 3:1)

This esteemed religious leader approached Jesus by night. Some biblical scholars say that he did so out of fear, while others say he just wanted to talk to Jesus without interruptions. Whatever the reason, we know that he came to Jesus and not Jesus coming to him. The first thing that Nick at

Night (reference to a television channel that airs old shows) did was to acknowledge:

1. Jesus came from God,
2. Jesus did signs,
3. These signs done by Jesus was because God was with Him.

   "...Rabbi (teacher), we know that you have come from God as a teacher, for no one can do these signs that you do unless God is with Him."
   (John 3:2)

Jesus did not acknowledge the truth of what Nick was saying; instead, He opened a dialogue about what it takes to see and enter the kingdom of God.

   "Jesus answered and said to him, 'Truly, Truly, I say to you, unless one is born again, *he cannot* see *the kingdom of God."*
   (John 3:3, emphasis mine)

BORN: gennaō (ghen-nah'-o)= to procreate (properly of the father, but by extension of the mother); figuratively to regenerate: - bear, beget, be born, bring forth, conceive, be delivered of, gender, make, spring. (Strong's)

AGAIN: anōthen (an'-o-then)=From G507; from above; by analogy from the first; by implication anew: - from above, again, from the beginning (very first), the top. G507:

anō (an'-o)= upward or on the top: - above, brim, high, up. (Strong's)

SEE: eidō (i'-do)= properly to see (literally or figuratively); by implication (in the perfect only) to know: - be aware, behold, X can (+ not tell), consider, (have) known (-ledge), look (on), perceive, see, be sure, tell, understand, wist, wot. (Strong's)

With the Strong's Concordance definitions in mind, John 3:3 reads like this:

> *"Jesus answered and said to him, 'Truly, Truly, I say to you, unless one is begat, brought forth, regenerated, conceived, delivered of, from above, anew, upward on the top, he cannot see, be aware, behold, consider, be sure, perceive, understand the kingdom of God."*
> (John 3:3, with Strong's definitions added)

If you are going to "see the kingdom of God," there must be some kind of transformation from the physical to the spiritual. This transformation of being born anew from above gives us the ability to see the kingdom of God. As we walk this earth in the physical, we can only see kingdoms of men and the d-evil, the prince of the power of the air, the god of this world. When we walk by faith and not by sight we begin to see things God's way, we begin to see God's kingdom.

KINGDOM: basileia (bas-il-i'-ah)=From G935; properly royalty, that is, (abstractly) rule, or (concretely) a realm (literally or figuratively): - kingdom, + reign. G935: basileus (bas-il-yooce')=Probably from G939 (through the notion of a foundation of power); a sovereign (abstractly, relatively or figuratively): - king. G939: basis (bas'-ece)=From bainō (to walk); a pace (base), that is, (by implication) the foot: - foot. (Strong's)

The extrapolation of the definition from Strong's is:

- Royalty
- Rule
- Realm
- Reign
- Foundation of power
- Sovereign
- Walk
- Pace
- Foot

In answer to Nick's affirmation of who Jesus is on Earth, Jesus lays out that Nick can see beyond what he is viewing in Jesus on Earth, but he will be able to see the kingdom if he is born from above instead of just being born on the physical earth. Again, John 3:3 reads like this:

"Jesus answered and said to him (Nick), 'Truly, Truly, I say to you (Nick) unless one is born from above, he cannot see the royalty, rule, realm, reign, foundation of power sovereign, walk, pace and foot of God.'"

(John 3:3, addition mine)

Jesus statement leads to another question by Nick.

"Nicodemus, said to Him, 'How can a man be born when

he is old? He cannot enter a second time into his mother's womb and be born, can he?'"

(John 3:4)

If we could only peer inside of Nick's brain and see a motion picture of what was playing in his mind. Picture a grown man trying to climb back into his mother's womb, so he can come out being born the second time physically. Jesus counters with what being born physically and being born spiritually means.

"Jesus answered, 'Truly, truly, I say to you, unless one is born of water and the Spirit he cannot enter into the kingdom of God.'"

(John 3:5)

"During pregnancy, your baby is surrounded and cushioned by a fluid-filled membranous sac called the amniotic sac. Typically, at the beginning of or during labor your membranes will rupture—also known as your water breaking. If your water breaks before labor starts, it's called premature rupture of membranes." (Mayo Clinic).

"…unless one is born of the fluid-filled amniotic sac, *the water breaking…"*

(John 3:5, paraphrase and emphasis mine0

So, you have to be born physical before you can be born spiritually. To be born again is not some reincarnation mumbo jumbo but a spiritual reality. This give and take, back-and-forth conversation at night between Nick and Jesus is very enlightening.

Jesus continues to speak and explain this physical and spiritual birth to Nick in John 3:5-8:

- Unless one is born of water and the Spirit, he cannot enter into the kingdom of God: Not only can you not *see* the kingdom, you cannot even *enter* into the kingdom.
- That which is born of the flesh is flesh (physical birth): This is the natural birth.
- That which is born of Spirit (Big S, the Holy Spirit) is spirit (little s, the human spirit): This is the supernatural birth where His *SUPER* comes on your natural.
- Do not be amazed that I said that you must be born again: This should not have been mind-blowing for Nick.
- The wind blows where it wishes and you heard the sound of it, but do not know where comes from and where it is going; so is everyone who is born of the Spirit: The Spirit is equated with the wind, which you cannot see with physical eyes, but only able to be seen as you walk by faith and not by sight.

NOTE: Many people who rely totally on their intellect and scientific research have told me that they cannot believe in something that they cannot see. I usually tell them to take a deep breath and tell me if they saw the oxygen coming in through their nares (aka nostrils) or did they see it exit out their mouths. Of course, the answer is, "No," at which time I inform them that not seeing the oxygen did not stop them from breathing or living. How often people use the same excuse with the things of God or things of the Spirit.

Nick's mind is blown as he responds.

"How can these things be?"

(John 3:9)

This question is reminiscent of Mary's response to Gabriel when he brought the news that she would be giving birth to Jesus.

"And Mary said to the angel, 'How can this be, since I am a virgin?'"

(Luke 1:34)

The expectation of Jesus was that Nick, who was a teacher of Israel, to understand these things. The conversation was about earthly things and heavenly things.

"Jesus answered and said to him, 'Are you the teacher of Israel, and do not understand these things.'"

(John 3:10)

Jesus was speaking about what He knows; about spiritual things. Not only is He speaking about what He knows, but also what He has seen. Jesus is giving out a witness.

WITNESS: marturia (mar-too-ree'-ah)=From G3144; evidence given (judicially or generally): - record, report, testimony, witness. G3144: martus (mar'-toos)=Of uncertain affinity; a witness (literally [judicially] or figuratively [generally]); by analogy a "martyr": - martyr, record, witness. (Strong's)

John—as he aged in the chronological sense and in the Lord—wrote in one of his epistles to the church about this thing called a witness. I imagine that he was thinking about the witness of spiritual things to Nick.

> *"What was from the beginning what we have heard, what we have seen with our eyes, what we beheld and our hands handled, concerning the Word of Life—and the life was manifested, and we have seen and bear witness and proclaim to you the eternal life, which was with the Father and was manifest to us—what we have seen and heard we proclaim to you also, that you may have fellowship with us; and indeed our fellowship is with the Father, and with His Son Jesus Christ. And these things we write, so that our joy may be made complete."*
>
> (1 John 1:1-4)

Standing before Nick was God in the flesh Who was in the beginning, Who was with God and Who was God. (John 1:1) God in the physical flesh and was telling him about spiritual things relating to physical things.

> *"If I told you earthly things and you do not believe; how shall you believe if I tell you heavenly things?"*
>
> (John 3:12)

In 1 Corinthians 2:9-14, the Apostle Paul explained this concept of how we can understand spiritual things.

- Things which eye has not seen and ear has not heard, and which have not entered the heart of man, all that

God has prepared for those who love Him (1 Corinthians 2:9)
- God *revealed things through the Spirit*; for the Spirit searches all things, even the depths of God. (1 Corinthians 2:10)
- Who knows the thoughts of man? The spirit (little s) of man that is the lamp of the Lord. (Pro-Verbs 20:27, 1 Corinthians 2:11)
- Who knows the thoughts of God? The Spirit (Big S) of God. (1 Corinthians 2:11)
- We have not received the spirit of the world (the natural system). (1 Corinthians 2:12)
- We have received the Spirit (Holy, Big S) who is from God. (1 Corinthians 2:12)
- We received the Spirit who is from God that we might know the things freely given to us by God. (1 Corinthians 2:12)
- We speak words not taught by human wisdom, but we speak words taught the Spirit (of God). (1 Corinthians 2:13)
- We speak a combination of spiritual thoughts and spiritual words. (1 Corinthians 2:13)
- A natural man does not accept the things of the Spirit of God because they are foolishness to him. (1 Corinthians 2:14)
- The natural man cannot understand the things of God because they are spiritually appraised. (1 Corinthians 2:14)

Nicodemus was having difficulty understanding spiritual things because he was reasoning with an earthly mind.

I you want to see and enter the Kingdom of God. If you want to understand heavenly things, you may have to understand earthly things. If you want to believe, you will have to understand His super coming on your natural. The bottom line is to believe in Him.

WRITTEN THAT YOU MAY BELIEVE

Lord, I believe that I can see and enter the Kingdom of God as I am born again, anew, from above.

4

THE COMING HOUR

"*But an hour is coming, and now is, when the true worshipers shall worship the Father in spirit and truth; for such people the Father seeks to be His worshipers.*"

(John 4:23)

Time is always moving. After each hour, there will be an hour coming in a twenty-four-hour sequence, and once completed the hour starts again. In the book of Acts, Jesus was described as a man on the move. He was always going about unless He was drawing away in prayer.

"*You know of Jesus of Nazareth how God anointed Him with the Holy Spirit and with power and how* He went about *doing good, and healing all who were oppressed by the d-evil for God was with Him.*"

(Acts 10:38, emphasis and addition mine)

The Pharisees had heard that Jesus was making and

baptizing more disciples than John (and that was a lot of disciples). Actually, Jesus was not baptizing them, but His disciples were baptizing them. (John 4:1-2)

Jesus was on the move as He left Judea and departed again into Galilee. If you flip in your Bible to the section where it has maps, or you do an internet search for images of Israel in Jesus' day, you will find the lay of the land where Jesus was going about in and doing good and healing all who were oppressed by the d-evil. If you draw a line from Judaea—where Jesus was departing from—up to Galilee, you will see the land of Samaria. To the right of that line you will see the Jordan River that connects with the Sea of Galilee.

THE SAMARITAN CONNECTION

The people of the land of Samaria were Jews who identified with the Northern Kingdom of Israel which had been exiled by the Assyrians. They believe that Mount Gerizim was the chosen place by God for worship. They also read only the Samaritan Pentateuch (the first five books of the Old Testament). After the exile, some had intermarried with Gentiles and there was lots of worship of foreign gods.

This led to animosity between the Jews of Jerusalem and the Samaritans. Which is why it was so dramatic that Jesus went straight into the heart of Samaria and then later gave instructions to the disciples to take the Gospel to Jerusalem, all Judea, Samaria, and unto the uttermost parts of the earth. (Acts 1:8)

The information about Samaria, the Samaritan people, and the conflict between the Jews and the Samaritans has been gleaned from various sources, including *The Zondervan*

Handbook of the Bible, Eerdmans' Handbook of the Bible, Holman Illustrated Bible Dictionary, IVP Handbook of Life in Bible Times.

The Samaritans were hated by the Jews, and whenever a 'good Jew' came to the borders of Samaria from the north or the south, he/she would cross the Jordan River and circumvent the land so as not to come into contact with the people. This is similar to how we avoid people of certain beliefs or character. We go out of the way to avoid the unclean so our cleanliness (man-made self-righteousness) would not be sullied. Jesus, God in the flesh, a teacher/Rabbi, Messiah was not that way. He crossed the boundary lines, went straight into the heart of the land and interacted with the people.

Jesus entered the Samaritan city of Sycar that was close to a parcel of ground that Jacob had given to his son Joseph. There was a well called Jacob's well and Jesus, being weary, was sitting by this well.

NOTE: I always find the humanity of Jesus interesting. The Son of God, God in the flesh, experienced the same things that we experience. He was weary and tired from His journey from Judea to Galilee. He had to make a pit stop to get some water. I can imagine that Jesus may have had to relive Himself or clear out His nose of boogers (walking in the sandy, dusty dry climate).

Jesus' disciples had gone away into the city to buy food. Jesus was sitting at the well, apparently not drinking any water at this point, when a woman of Samaria (aka The Samaritan Woman) came to the well to draw some water. Jesus spoke to the woman (gasp) and said,

"Give me a drink."

(John 4:7)

NOTE: Now to me this sounds kind of brusque without even a please.

Now the woman knew that Jesus was a Jew and she knew both of their social status; Jesus a Jew and her being a woman and a Samaritan woman at that. John fills in the blanks when he writes,

"For Jews have no dealings with Samaritans."
(John 4:9)

"Jesus answered and said to her, 'If you knew the gift of God and Who it is who says to you, 'give me a drink', you would have asked Him, and He would have given you living water."
(John 4:10)

Jesus' response turned the tables on the Samaritan woman.

- Jesus is thirsty (physically)
- Jesus demands a drink of water (physical)
- She questions Him talking to her being a woman and a Samaritan.
- Jesus responds back with a statement that indicates His true purpose for talking about water.
- Instead of her giving Him water, He was prepared to give her spiritual water. Jesus was talking living water (spiritual) and she was talking about physical water.

NOTE: Jesus was talking about the gift of God, Himself. At this point she is still on the physical plane talking about physical, wet water.

> *"She said to Him, "Sir, You have nothing to draw with and the well is deep; where then do You get that living water? You are not greater our father Jacob, are You who gave us the well, and drank of it himself, and his sons, and his cattle?"*
> (John 4:11-12)

She proceeded to educate Jesus on history as she speaks of Jacob at whose well they were talking.

Jesus begins to educate her about water and wells in John 4:13-14:

- Everyone who drinks of this water (Jacob's well) will thirst again.
- Whoever drinks of the water that I give (living water) shall become in him (new location for a new well) a well of water springing up to eternal life.

Her response was a request for Jesus to give her this water He was talking about so that she:

1. would not have to come to Jacob's well to draw water and,
2. so she will not be thirsty. (John 4:15)

Jesus begins to go beyond living water, but the need for living water in John 4:13-14. At this time, the woman requests the water that Jesus spoke about. In John 4:15:

- Sir, give me this water so I will not be thirsty.
- Sir, give me this water so I will not have to come all the way here to draw the water.

Jesus instructed her to call her husband and tell him to come to the well. Jesus begins to peel back the hidden layers in the onion of her life and find the core to her real problem which was not just water. In John 4:16-19 we see:

- I have no husband.
- Jesus knew (operating in the word of wisdom/knowledge) that she had five husbands in the past.
- Jesus knew that the one she had now was not her husband (apparently living with him).
- At this point, she realized that something was amiss. She stated that she perceived that Jesus was a prophet.

When this woman realized that she was not just dealing with an ordinary Jew, but that He was a prophet, she shifted the conversation to religion. How often do we retreat to religion when we are confronted about our lifestyle?

> *"Our fathers worshiped in this mountain; and you people (the Jews) say that in Jerusalem is the place where men ought to worship."*
>
> (John 4:20, addition mine)

WORSHIP: proskuneō (pros-koo-neh'-o)= (meaning to kiss, like a dog licking his master's hand); to fawn or crouch to, that is, (literally or figuratively) prostrate oneself in homage (do reverence to, adore): - worship. (Strong's)

The woman at the well now has opened the door for some truth. IN her religious pretense, she thought that she could deflect focus from her wanton lifestyle. But now Jesus is bringing her face-to-face with what true worship looks like.

> *"Jesus said to her, 'Woman, believe Me, an hour us coming when neither in this mountain, nor in Jerusalem, shall you worship the Father. You worship that which you do not know; for we worship that which we know; for salvation is from the Jews."*
>
> (John 4:21-22, emphasis mine)

She is about to see that it is not about a matter of the location of worship, but it is all about a matter of the heart. Jesus is about to reveal to her where true worshipers worship the Father.

> *"But an hour is coming, and now is, when the true worshipers shall worship the Father in spirit and truth; for such people the Father seeks to be His worshipers. God is spirit; and those who worship Him must worship in spirit and truth."*
>
> (John 4:23-24)

LOCATION OF TRUE WORSHIP BY TRUE WORSHIPPERS

- In spirit (little s). True worship is found within us. "The spirit of man is the lamp of the LORD, Searching all the innermost parts of his being." (Pro-Verbs 20:27)
- In truth. Truth is the Word of God. "Sanctify them (disciples/followers) in truth; Thy Word is truth." (John 17:17)

The good news is this; we are not limited by location, style, denomination, or physical buildings. Our bodies are the temple of the Holy Ghost and the Spirit of God dwells within us. (1 Corinthians 3:16, 1 Corinthians 6:19) We can be on a mountain or in a city, if we are true worshipers we worship in the spirit and according to His Word. No longer are we limited in our worship. If we truly believe that truth, our worship takes place 7/24/365 wherever we are located.

NOTE: If we really believed that our bodies are the dwelling place for the Holy Spirit—and that wherever we go the Holy Spirit is there—we might not do certain things that we think are hidden from God, but realize He is right there with us.

WRITTEN THAT YOU MAY BELIEVE

Lord, I believe that Your Holy Spirit within my human spirit gives me the opportunity to worship You in the truth of the Word of God.

5

WHO IS THE MAN?

"They asked him, 'Who is the man who said to you 'Take up your pallet, and walk?'"

(John 5:12)

Jesus is continuing in the Modus Operandi that He began after being baptized in the Jordan River and anointed by the Father with the Holy Ghost and power (dynamic ability). (Matthew 3:11-17, Matthew 4:23-25, Acts 10:38) Jesus:

- Went about
- Doing good
- Healing all who were oppressed by the d-evil
- God was with Him (Immanuel, God with us)
- Taught in their synagogues
- Declared/Proclaimed the Kingdom
- Healed the sick

Jesus had gone up to Jerusalem during a feast, most likely

Pentecost. He went to an area by the sheep gate that had a pool named Bethesda. There were five porches (porticos) at this pool where there was a multitude of those who were sick, blind, lame, and withered. Jesus saw one man there and knew he had been sick for thirty-eight years.

NOTE: The Word does not indicate that Jesus knew this man personally but knew (perceived) that he had been in that condition of sickness for a long time.

Jesus asked this man a question, that to some may seem odd or even insensitive.

> *"…do you wish to get well?"*

(John 5:6)

What kind of question is that? Doesn't everyone who is sick want to get well? This is true especially if they have been sick for many years or even all their lives. Sometimes we have been in our condition (sick, beaten down in poverty, trapped in addictions) for so long that it becomes second nature to us. We feel that it is our lot in life; or that it is God's will for us; or that we deserve whatever it is and brought it on ourselves.

That is, until Jesus comes to us and asks us, "Do you wish to get well? Do you wish to be delivered from your bondages and addictions? Do you wish to be delivered out from underneath the thumb of poverty?"

This man who had been sick stated what he had experienced for thirty-eight years.

> *"The sick man answered Him, 'Sir, I have no man to put me into the pool when the water is stirred up, but while I*

am coming, another steps down before men.'"

(John 5:7)

NOTE: The story is that an angel would come down in a certain season and stir up the water and those who stepped into the stirred waters was made well, healed from whatever disease with which they were afflicted. The man's excuse was that someone stepped in front of him and prevented him from receiving his healing. What excuse do you have for not receiving your healing?

Jesus went beyond his excuses and spoke specifically to the mountain of his sickness (Mark 11:22-25)

"Jesus said to him, "Arise, take up your pallet and walk. And immediately the man became well, took up his pallet and began to walk. Now it was the Sabbath on that day."

(John 5:8-9)

The Law of Moses prohibited work on the Sabbath. Of course, the religious people took that law several steps further. They had all kinds of reasons why the man should not be healed. In John 5:10, we see the Jews were saying to him:

- It is the Sabbath.
- It is not permissible for you to carry your pallet.

The cured man, the healed man, the one who had not been able to walk for thirty-eight years, had only one answer for them.

"But he answered them, 'He who made me well was the

one who said to me, "Take up your pallet and walk."'
(John 5:11)

The question from the Jews was,

"…who is the man who said to you, 'Take up your pallet, and walk?"'
(John 5:12

While the cured/healed man did not know the name, his answer to this question was Jesus. Later the man encountered the One Who had healed him and returned to the Jews and told them that it was Jesus. The cause-and-effect of learning the name of Jesus (John 5:15-18) was:

- The Jews were persecuting Jesus for doing these things (healing) on the Sabbath day.
- The Jews were seeking all the more to kill Him.
- Jesus was not only breaking the Sabbath.
- Jesus was also calling God His own Father.
- Jesus was making Himself equal to God.

The religious leaders asked the questions, but they did not realize that the answer was going to turn their worlds upside down. It is like a dog chasing a car but can only bite the tires when he finally catches it. They knew the name of the man, but all they could do wass bite at him like a dog in a feeding frenzy.

When you receive Jesus, or when Jesus heals and delivers you, be ready for people to ask you, "Who is the man who said to you…?" Then be ready for their reaction.

Follow Jesus' order to you:

> *"Afterward Jesus found him (the healed man) in the temple, and said to him, 'Behold,* you have become well; *do not sin any more so that nothing worse may befall you."*
> (John 5:14, addition and emphasis mine)

Jesus came for a purpose and that purpose was to destroy the works of the d-evil, (1 John 3:8, addition mine) that included sin and sickness.

> *"Which is easier to say "'Your sins have been forgiven you, or to say, 'rise and walk?"*
> (Matthew 9:5, Mark 2:9, Luke 5:23)

WRITTEN THAT YOU MAY BELIEVE

Lord, I believe that You can do both; heal my sicknesses and forgive my sins.

6

FULL OF WONDERFUL BREAD

"Jesus therefore lifting up His eyes, and seeing that a great multitude was coming to Him, said to Philip, 'Where are we to buy bread that these may eat?' And this He was saying to test him; for He Himself knew what He was intending to do."

(John 6:5-6)

In the previous chapter, we see that Jesus was doing works and taking the opportunity to reveal His connection to the Father. In John 1:1-4, it is revealed that Jesus was the Word, and the Word was with God, and the Word was God. (For full details read the first chapter of this book and John 1:1-14 again.) This information made those who was religious angry, seeking to kill Jesus.

Remember that this book was,

"...written that you may believe."

(John 20:31)

So everything that Jesus did and said was by divine design, to break through unbelief and bring us to where we have to make a choice to believe.

> *"And the Father who sent Me, He has borne witness of Me. You have neither heard His voice at any time, nor seen His form. And you do not have His word abiding in you, for you do not believe Him whom He sent. You search the Scriptures, because you think that in them you have eternal life; and it is these that bear witness of Me; and you are unwilling to come to Me, that you may have life."*
> (John 5:37-40)

The key to breaking from religious traditions is hinged on going beyond believing Moses but believing Jesus. Moses only pointed to Jesus. Jesus underscores the need to believe and to have the abiding word if you are going to be able to believe. Let us see how true belief brings us into relationship with Jesus. In John 5:38-47:

- You do not believe Him (The Father) Whom He (The Father) sent (Jesus),
- How can you believe, when you receive glory from one another (religious people), and do not seek the glory that is from the one and only God (The Father)?
- If you believed Moses, you would believe Me (Jesus); for he (Moses) wrote of Me (Jesus)
- But if you do not believe his (Moses') writings, how will you believe My (Jesus) words.

NOTE: I know that in Chapter Six of this book we should

be in Chapter Six of John, but John, Chapter Five, sets us up for Chapter Six for this book.

> *"After these things (Jesus explaining about believing in Him) Jesus went to the other side of the Sea of Galilee (or Tiberias). And a large crowd (great multitude) was following Him, because they were seeking the signs (attesting miracles) which He was performing on those who were sick."*
> (John 6:1-2, addition mine)

Jesus proceeded to go up on the mountain and sat down with His disciples. The Passover (a feast of the Jew's commemorating the passing over of the death angel in Egypt of those who had a lamb slaughter and the blood over their door) was near. A feast meant that food was consumed. Jesus looked up and saw the multitude coming to Him and He turned to Philip and asked him,

> *"Where are we to buy bread that these may eat?"*
> (John 6:5)

I am sure that Jesus was concerned about feeding these people, but according to this passage, Jesus was testing Philip and had intentions for something other than finding food. If you look at all the other Gospels, you will see Jesus taking opportunities from everyday life to teach about spiritual principles of the Kingdom of God.

> *"And this He was saying to test him; for He Himself knew what He was intending to do."*
> (John 6:6, emphasis mine)

Philip, still thinking on earthly terms, was trying to figure out how they would buy enough bread with two hundred denarii (one denarius represented one day's wage). Andrew, Peter's brother, was thinking on earthly terms also. In John 6:9-13 the feeding of the five thousand took place like this.

- Andrew knew that there was a lad who had five barley loaves and two fish.
- Andrew questions, "…but what are these for so many people?"
- Jesus told them to direct the 5,000 people sit down on the grass.
- Jesus took the bread and gave thanks and distributed to those who were seated.
- Jesus did the same thing with the fish.
- The 5,000 had as much as they wanted, to the point of being filled.
- Jesus told the disciples to gather the leftover fragments that nothing be lost.
- They gathered them up, filled twelve baskets with fragments which were left over.

The people not only ate the bread and fish, but they saw the sign which Jesus had performed. They said:

"…this is of a truth the Prophet who is to come into the world."

(John 6:14)

Jesus had intentions (John 6:6) and knew the intentions of the 5,000 people, which was, "to come and take Him by force, to make Him king…" (John 6:15) Jesus withdrew by Himself to the mountain.

Thus far, we see that Jesus was testing Philip when He asked him where they were going to get bread to feed the people. We have also seen that Jesus was intending to do something, which appears to have been supplying the needs of the people, by multiplying the lad's five loaves of bread and two fishes to feed 5,000 people, and have food leftover. I think that Jesus' intentions were beyond the supply, but as He did often, utilized things to set them up for the deeper meaning of bread.

> *"I am the bread of life."*
>
> (John 6:48)

The ones who ate the bread and fish followed Jesus, seeking a sign from Him, as if feeding 5,000 people on five loaves of bread and two fish was not enough of a sign.

NOTE: Isn't that how we are (or at least I am); always wanting more and more never being filled like my belly, but an hour later wanting more?

> *"They said therefore to Him, 'What then do You do for a sign, that we may see and believe in You? What work do You perform? Our fathers ate the manna in the wilderness; as it is written, He gave them bread out of heave to eat.'"*
>
> (John 6:30-31)

Jesus responded with what I think was His original intention. (John 6:6) Jesus took their mention of manna and then revealed the true manna/bread was actually Himself. Jesus answered them in their quest for bread in John 6:32-35:

- Truly, truly I say to you *it is not Moses* who has given you bread out of heaven.
- But it is *My Father who gives you* the true bread out of heaven.
- The *bread of God* is that which *comes down out of heaven* and *gives life to the world*

The people wanted this bread.

> *"They said therefore to Him, 'Lord, evermore give us this bread."*
>
> (John 6:34)

Jesus defined and clarified about the bread that He was speaking about.

> *"Jesus said to them, 'I am the bread of life; he who comes to Me shall not hunger, and He who believes in Me shall never thirst."*
>
> (John 6:35)

Manna was a temporary thing, but the Bread of Life is forever.

> *"Truly, truly, I say to you he who believes has eternal life. I am the bread of life. Your fathers ate manna in the wilderness, and they died. This is the bread which comes down out of heaven, so that one may eat of it and not die. I am the living bread that comes down out of heaven; if any*

one eats of this bread he shall live forever; and the bread also which I shall give for the life of the world is my flesh."

(John 6:47-51)

Jesus then shocked them by comparing His flesh to bread and His blood for drink. Read John 6:51-58 for full details. The bottom line for believers is this,

"This is the bread which came down out of heaven; not as the fathers ate, and died, he who eats this bread shall live forever."

(John 6:58)

WRITTEN THAT YOU MAY BELIEVE

Lord, I believe that manna was temporary, but You are forever, and if You are forever, then I will live forever.

7

FLOWING RIVERS

"He who believes in Me, as the Scripture said, 'From his innermost being shall flow rivers of living waters.'"
(John 7:38)

On Jesus' thirty-three years on Earth, three of those were spent going about, doing good, and healing all who were oppressed by the d-evil. (Acts 10:38) Jesus came for the purpose of destroying the works of the d-evil. (1 John 3:8) He was anointed with the Spirit to preach, proclaim, and demonstrate the will of God on earth as it is in heaven. (Luke 4:17-21) His modus operandi was to: (1) teach in their synagogues; (2) declare the kingdom; (3) heal the sick. (Matthew 4:23-25)

Among the people, there were many responses to all of this. Some loved Him and pressed in around Him to get close others plotted against Him. (John 7:8-36) The last day of the great feast was when Jesus spoke of living waters.

> "...the Jews had a ceremony of carrying water from the Pool of Siloam and pouring it into a silver basin by the altar of burnt offering each day for the first seven days of the Feast of Booths. On the eight day this was not done, making Christ's offer of the water of eternal life from Himself even more startling."
>
> (Ryrie study notes)

NOTE: The Feast of Booths was one of three pilgrimages of the Jewish year, occurring in the autumn after harvest. For seven days of the festival, the Jews dwelt in booths made of the boughs of trees. This was also known as the Feast of Tabernacles to commemorate Israel's wilderness experience. It was on the last day of this festival that Jesus stood up.

The last day (the eight day) of the great feast (Feast of Booths) Jesus stood up. Jesus had been seated, and when He stood, He was the center of attention. Jesus cried out. He had to cry out to be heard among the people to get their attention.

> "...if anyone is thirsty (for water) come to Me and drink."
>
> (John 7:37)

Everyone knew what it meant to be thirsty in the physical realm, but Jesus was talking about a different realm. It was this kind of talk from Jesus that made the religious leaders mad and wanting to plot against Him.

> "He who believes in Me, as the Scripture said, from his innermost being will flow rivers of living water."
>
> (John 7:38, Isaiah 44:3, Isaiah 55:1, Isaiah 58:11)

Jesus was a Scripture man and knew the Word of God.

"For I will pour out water on the thirsty land and streams on the dry ground; I will pour out My Spirit on your offspring and My blessing on your descendants."
(Isaiah 44:3)

"Ho, everyone who thirsts, come to the waters; and you who have no money come, buy and eat come, buy wine and milk without money and without cost."
(Isaiah 55:1)

"And the Lord will continually guide you, and satisfy your desire in scorched places, and give strength to your bones; and you will be like a watered garden, and like a spring of water whose water does not fail."
(Isaiah 58:11)

NOTE: I have always thought of this as the rivers flowing out of me. I have always thought of it as The Holy Spirit flowing out of me. While that may be true, in this scene, I see Jesus announcing to the people that there is a river flowing out of Him and that river is the Holy Spirit.

The flow comes from within the deep recesses of the innermost being. Notice that it is not just a river, but it is river(s), plural of living water. This water is not like waters of a stagnant pool or a Dead Sea; but the waters are living, alive.

LIVING: zaō (dzah'-o)=A primary verb; to live (literally or

figuratively): - life (-time), (a-) live (-ly), quick. (Strong's)

WATER: hudōr hudatos (hoo'-dor, hoo'-dat-os)=From the base of G5205; water (as if rainy) literally or figuratively: - water. (Strong's)

Jesus then defined Who He was speaking about.

"But this He spoke of the Spirit…"

(John 7:39)

This Spirit Who He was talking about had not yet been given, because He had not yet been glorified after His death, burial, resurrection, and ascension back to the Father. This Spirit would be poured out from the Father later in the Book of Acts as they waited in obedience in Jerusalem. (Luke 24:49, Acts 1:4-5, Acts 1:8, Acts 2:1-13)

You can believe for sure that Jesus loves you and that on the cross He provided the cancellation of the debt that you owed (Colossians 2:14 He became a curse on the tree, so you would not have to be cursed. Galatians 3:13, Deuteronomy 21:23) You can also believe that when He went back to the Father, and that He would send the same Holy Spirit (John 14:16) that flowed out of His innermost being into your body would be a temple for the Holy Spirit and flow out to others as you move in Him.

WRITTEN THAT YOU MAY BELIEVE

Lord, I believe that with You dwelling in me, that as rivers flow out of You, they will flow out of me.

FREE INDEED

"So if the Son makes you free, you will be free indeed."
(John 8:36)

FREE: Eleutheros (el-yoo'-ther-os)= unrestrained (to go at pleasure), that is, (as a citizen) not a slave (whether freeborn or manumitted), or (generally) exempt (from obligation or liability): - free (man, woman), at liberty. (Strong's)

INDEED: ontōs (on'-toce)= really: - certainly, clean, indeed, of a truth, verily. (Strong's)

I like the idea of being unrestrained, without any doubts, to really, really, really being free.

Jesus once again was telling people Who He was and what He would be doing. He had been demonstrating the power over the oppression of the d-evil by forgiving the woman of her sins whom the religious leaders had accused of adultery.

In reality, she was only a tool being used by religious leaders to entrap Jesus. From John 8:12-29, we see a sample of the back-and-forth dialogue between religious people and Jesus.

- Jesus said, "I am the light of the world, he who follows Me shall not walk in the darkness, but shall have the light."
- The Pharisees said, "You are witness of Yourself; Your witness is not true."
- Jesus said, "Even if I bear witness of Myself, My witness is true; for I know where I came from and where I am going; but you do not know where I come from, or where I am going."
- Jesus continues the thought that He started. "You people judge according to the flesh; I am not judging any one. But even if I do judge, My Judgment is true; for I am not alone in it, but I and He who sent Me. Even in your law it has been written, that the testimony of two men is true. I am He who bears witness of Myself, and the Father who sent Me bears witness of Me."
- The Pharisees continue their rebuttal of what Jesus just said. "Where is your Father?
- Jesus responds back. "You know neither Me, nor my Father; if you knew Me, you would know My Father also.

NOTE: Jesus spoke these words in the treasury, as He taught in the temple; and no one seized Him, because His hour had not yet come. (John 8:20)

- Jesus continued. "I go away, and you shall not seek Me, and shall die in your sin; where I am going, you cannot come."
- The Jews responded with questions among themselves. "Surely He will not kill Himself, will He, since He says 'Where I am going, you cannot come.'"
- Jesus told them, "You are from below, I am from above; you are of this world; I am not of this world…you shall die in your sins."
- The Pharisees asked the million-dollar question. "Who are You?"
- Jesus answered them, "I have many things to speak and judge concerning, but He who sent me is true; and the things which I heard from Him these I speak to the world."

NOTE: The Pharisees did not realize that He had been speaking to them about the Father.

Jesus told them,

"When you lift up the Son of Man, then you will know that I am He, and I do nothing on My own initiative, but I speak these things as the Father taught Me and He who sent Me is with Me; He has not left me alone, for I always do the things that are pleasing to Him."

NOTE: As Jesus and the Pharisees went back and forth, there were the Jews listening to this ping pong dialogue. The cause-and-effect was that many came to believe in Him, Jesus, God in the flesh.

"As he spoke these things many came to believe in Him."
(John 8:30)

Jesus then shifted His Word from the Pharisees to those who had believed in Him. I am thinking that there was a mixture of believers, from religious leaders to the common everyday Jew.

NOTE: Remember, Jesus was a Jew.
- Jesus told these Jewish believers, "If you abide in My word, then you are truly disciples of Mine; and you shall know the truth, and the truth shall make you free."

NOTE: Apparently believing was just the beginning. There was more to follow if they wanted to be free. The key word is if. If you do something, something will happen, if you don't do something, something will not happen. Let's see the "if factor".

ABIDE/CONTINUE: menō (men'-o)=A primary verb; to stay (in a given place, state, relation or expectancy): - abide, continue, dwell, endure, be present, remain, stand, tarry (for), X thine own. (Strong's)

DISCIPLE: mathētēs (math-ay-tes')=From G3129; a learner, that is, pupil: - disciple. G3129: manthanō (man-than'-o)=Prolonged from a primary verb, another form of which is used as an alternate in certain tenses; to learn (in any way): - learn, understand. (Strong's)

NOTE: The abiding in the Word will make you a disciple. If you don't abide in the Word, you will only be a believer. The next step, as you go from a believer to a disciple, brings you to a position of knowing the Truth. Now you are ready to be made free.

All of this should be good news, but the believers looked

on it as bad news and something they could not relate to, since they had a religious heritage.

> *"They answered Him, 'We are Abraham's offspring, and have never yet been enslaved to anyone; how is it that You say, 'You shall become free?'"*
>
> (John 8:33)

NOTE: This is the classic moment where they could not admit that they were in bondage. It is hard to be set free from something that you are convinced that you are not, or you are not conscious about.

Jesus cuts to the heart of the matter of what binds us; sin.

> *"Jesus answered them, 'Truly, truly, I say to you, everyone who commits sin is the slave of sin, and the slave does not remain in the house forever; the Son does remain forever.'"*
>
> (John 8:34-35)

> *Paul spoke of this in the Book of Romans. "For sin shall not be master over you, for you are not under law, but under grace."*
>
> (Romans 6:14)

> *Jesus underscored this grace when He declared, "If therefore the Son shall make you free, you shall be free indeed."*
>
> (John 8:36)

The process is:

- Believe in Him (trust in, cling to, rely upon)
- Continue/Abide in His Words (renew your mind and take up residence in the Word)
- Know the truth (the Word is Truth, John 17:17)
- Become free indeed (released from the power of sin, without a doubt)

WRITTEN THAT YOU MAY BELIEVE

Lord, I believe You, I believe Your Words, I believe Your Truth and I believe that when You set me free, I will be free indeed (without a doubt).

DISPLAYED WORKS

"Jesus answered, 'It was neither that this man sinned, nor his parents; but in order that the works of God be displayed in him."

(John 9:3)

NOTE: Warning, this is a long one, but it is worth reading until the end.

As we have seen in other chapters, Jesus was going about doing good and healing all who were sick or oppressed by the d-evil. (Acts 10:38, Matthew 4:23-24) As He did His thing, His followers had questions. As Jesus was on the go, they passed by a man who had been blind from birth. The disciples had questions:

- Who sinned?
- The man, or
- His parents?

The idea was that God's judgment came on the man because of sin.

SINNED: hamartanō (ham-ar-tan'-o)= properly to miss the mark (and so not share in the prize), that is, (figuratively) to err, especially (morally) to sin: - for your faults, offend, sin, trespass. (Strong's)

- Miss the mark
- Not share in the prize
- Err
- To sin morally
- Faults
- Offend
- Trespass

> *"As it is written, 'There is none righteous, no not one.'"*
> (Romans 3:10)

> *"For all have sinned and fall short of the glory of God."*
> (Romans 3:23)

> *"Therefore, just as through one man sin entered into the world and so death spread to all men, because all have sinned."*
> (Romans 5:12)

> *"Now all these things are from God, Who reconciled us to Himself through Christ, and gave us the ministry of reconciliation, namely, that God was in Christ reconciling the world to Himself, not counting their trespasses against*

them, and He has committed to us the word of reconciliation. Therefore, we are ambassadors for Christ, as though God were entreating through us; we beg you on behalf of Christ, be reconciled to God. He made Him who knew no sin to be sin on our behalf that we might become the righteousness of God in Him."

(2 Corinthians 5:18-21)

As John 9 states that this man was born blind from birth, it appears to me that he did not have a lot time to sin and be struck with blindness. Of course, some would say that we are sinners from birth (Romans 5:12) so he qualifies for blindness. Not likely!

"You know of Jesus of Nazareth, how God anointed Him (Jesus) with the Holy Ghost and power (dynamic ability) and how He went about doing good (not bad) and healing all (all means all) who were oppressed (put down) by the d-evil, for God was with Him, (Immanuel, God with us)."

(Acts 10:38, addition mine)

Combine that with 1 John 3:8, where we see that Jesus came (from the Father) for a purpose and that purpose was to,

"...destroy the works of the d-evil."

(1 John 3:8, addition mine)

Sin and sickness is the work of the d-evil, and when you read Matthew, Mark, Luke, and John, you see Jesus going about, teaching in the synagogues, declaring/proclaiming the Kingdom of God, and healing and delivering the people from the works and oppression of the d-evil.

With this in mind, we see that Jesus answers the disciples' question about who committed the sin that caused this man's blindness.

> *"Jesus answered, 'It was neither that this man sinned nor his parents; but it was in order (the reason)* that the works of God might be displayed in him."
> (John 9:3, emphasis and addition mine)

WORKS: Ergon (er'-gon)=From ergō (a primary but obsolete word; to work); toil (as an effort or occupation); by implication an act: - deed, doing, labour, work. (Strong's)

> *"We must work the works of Him who sent Me, as long as it is day; night is coming, when no man can work."*
> (John 9:4)

NOTE: The works of healing and deliverance were the works of God the Father Who sent Jesus to do His works. If we could ever get it in our minds that sickness and sin are not the works of God, but the works of the d-evil would not be pulled in two different directions concerning healing. When we realize that Jesus came for the purpose of destroying the works of the d-evil, we would not accept anything that happens to us as the will (wish/desire) of God.

NOTE: In the gospels of Matthew, Mark, Luke, and John, there were around forty cases of Jesus doing good works, and in every case, it was *not* God, or people's own fault, or the fault of others, that made them sick. It was oppression of the d-evil. Jesus was destroying the works of the d-evil and not God making people sick.

After answering their question, and declaring the kingdom of works, Jesus began to work. (John 8:6-7) Jesus:

- Spit on the ground
- Made clay of the spittle
- Applied the clay to the blind man's eyes
- Told the blind man to go and wash in the pool of Siloam ('Siloam' means *sent*)

The-cause-and-effect of Jesus' odd methods, and the man's obedience, was healing of the man's eyes. He came back from his journey of obedience seeing.

People began to talk about what happened and asked questions:

- Is not this the one used to sit and beg?
- This is he.
- No, but he is like him.
- The man kept saying, "I am the one."
- The people continued with questions, "How then were your eyes open?"

"And He answered, 'The man who is called Jesus made clay, and anointed my eyes, and said to me go to Siloam and wash. So I went away and washed and I received sight."
(John 9:11)

NOTE: Jesus was nowhere to be found to verify that it was He who had healed the man. The healed man (a.k.a. the blind man from birth, a.k.a. he who was formerly blind) was brought to the Pharisees. The healed man answered their questions about receiving his sight and told his story again. He/the man who healed me:

1. applied clay to my eyes;
2. I washed; and
3. I see.

Now like Pharisees tend to do, they got all religious and start accusing Jesus of not being from God. Why? Because He does not keep the Sabbath. Others were saying, "How can a man who is a sinner perform such signs?" So, a division ensues among them.

They asked the blind man what he had to say about this man Who opened his eyes. The man said, "He is a prophet." Of course, the Jews did not believe it, so they called in witnesses; the man's parents. They quizzed them about if he was their son and if so, how does he now see. The parents responded:

- We know that he is our son.
- We know that he was born blind.
- We know that he now sees.
- We do not know how he now sees.
- We do not know who opened his eyes.
- Ask him (their son), he is of age.
- They said this because they were afraid of the Jews.
- The Jews had already agreed that if anyone should confess Him [Jesus] to be the Christ, he should be put out of the synagogue.

- It was for this reason they told the Pharisees that he was of age and to ask him.

"So a second time they called the man who had been blind, and said to him, 'Give glory to God; we know that this man is a sinner. He therefore answered, 'Whether He is a sinner, I do not know; one thing I do know, that, whereas I was blind, now I see."

(John 9:25)

The questioning continues,

"What did He do to you? How did He open your eyes?"

(John 9:26)

His response is classic,

"I told you already, and you did not listen; why do you want to hear it again? You do not want to become His disciples too, do you?"

(John 9:27)

The back-and-forth question and answering continues:

- The Pharisees reviled him.
- The Pharisees told that he was a disciple of Jesus and that they were disciples of Moses.
- The Pharisees knew that God spoke to Moses but for "this man" we do not know where He is from.
- The healed man spoke of an amazing thing that they did not know where He is from, and yet He opened my eyes.

- The healed man continues that we know that God does not heard sinners; but if any one who is God-fearing, and does His will, He hears him.
- The healed man states that, since the beginning of time, it has never been heart that any one opened the eyes of a person born blind.
- The blind man states that, if this man were not from God, He could do nothing.
- The Pharisees turn it back on the healed man. "You were born entirely in sin, and you are teaching us?"
- The Pharisees then put him out of the synagogue.

Jesus heard about what had happened and sought out the healed man (John 9:35) and asked him the question that I believe that He asks all of us.

> "...*do you* believe *in the Son of Man?*"
> (John 9:36, emphasis mine)

The blind man responds,

> "*Who is He, Lord that I may* believe *in Him?*"
> (John 9:36, emphasis mine)

Jesus tells him,

> "...*You have both seen Him, and He is the one who is talking to you.*"
> (John 9:37)

The healed man responds with the correct answer,

"And he said, 'Lord, I believe,' and he worshiped Him."
(John 9:38)

"And Jesus said, 'For judgment I came into this world, that those who do not see may see; and that those who see may become blind.'"
(John 9:39)

"Those of the Pharisees who were with Him heard these things, and said to Him, 'We are not blind too, are we?'"
(John 9:40)

"Jesus said to them, 'If you were blind, you would have no sin; but now you say, "we see;" your sin remains.'"
(John 9:41)

Wow! Talk about high drama. Jesus took the healing of a blind man and the attacks by the Pharisees and turned it into a lesson on sin.

WRITTEN THAT YOU MAY BELIVE

Lord, I also believe, and I worship You as You have dealt with my sins. I believe that Your grace is truly amazing.

10

ABUNDANT LIFE

"The thief comes only to steal, and kill, and destroy; I came that they might have life, and might have it abundantly."
(John 10:10)

ABUNDANT: Perissos (per-is-sos')= in the sense of beyond; superabundant (in quantity) or superior (in quality); by implication excessive; adverb (with G1537) violently; neuter (as noun) preeminence: - exceeding abundantly above, more abundantly, advantage, exceedingly, very highly, beyond measure, more, superfluous, vehement [-ly]. (Strong's)

LIFE: zōē (dzo-ay')=From G2198; life (literally or figuratively): - life (-time). G2198: zaō (dzah'-o)=A primary verb; to live (literally or figuratively): - life (-time), (a-) live (-ly), quick. (Strong's)

What a wonderful picture of our choices. We can align

with the thief (a.k.a. the d-evil) or we can align with Jesus. I don't know about you, but I do not want to have someone take my blessings, kill my dreams, and destroy my life. I would much rather have a life and live it. To live a life that goes beyond into the realm of superabundance and is superior. I want a life that is exceeding abundantly above and is beyond measure.

> *"Now to Him who is able to do far more abundantly beyond all that we ask or think, according to the power that works within us, to Him be the glory in the church and in Christ Jesus to all generations forever and ever. Amen."*
> (Ephesians 3:20-21)

Remember that the Bible was not written with chapters and numbers. As you read it, there may be a period of a thought, and then you enter into the next chapter, but the thought may flow into the next chapter. This is true between Chapter Nine and Chapter Ten.

Jesus had just told the Pharisees that they were not believers and worshipers, but they were blinded by their sins. Jesus continued with images and metaphors about sheep, shepherds, and sheep folds. Jesus identified Himself, "the door." The door is the entrance way into the sheep folds. The words door or doorkeeper appears five times in Chapter Ten.

1. John 10:1 He does not enter by the door into the fold.
2. John 10:2 He who enters by the door is a shepherd to the sheep.
3. John 10:3 The doorkeeper opens the door and the sheep hear his voice.

4. John 10:7 I am the door of the sheep.
5. John 10:9 I am the door.

"I am the door; if anyone enters through Me, he shall be saved, and shall go in and out and find pasture."
(John 10:9)

Jesus then compares the thief to the good shepherd, Who is also the door.

"The thief comes only to steal, and kill, and destroy; I came that they might have life, and might have it abundantly."
(John10:10)

NOTE: Many Christians, theologians, pastors have identified this thief as the d-evil. I have personally used John 10:10 to identify the d-evil as the one who is out to kill, steal, and destroy us. I still believe that, but as I read the flow and context of Jesus' thoughts that He is speaking of the Pharisees who are blinded in their sins as the ones who are trying to enter into the sheepfold by other means instead of by the door.

Jesus identifies them as:

- Pharisees who are blinded by sin
- Thief
- Strangers
- Robbers
- Stealers
- Killers

- Destroyers
- Hireling
- Wolf
- Not a shepherd

Whoever this thief is—whether the Pharisees or the d-evil—the bottom line is that their purpose is to prevent the sheep from having an abundant life, but steal (blessings), kill (vision), and destroy (life).

Once again, there arose a division among the Jews because of Jesus' words.

NOTE: Have you notice that this issue continues to rise repeatedly?

"There arose a division among the Jews because of these words."

(John 10:19)

According to John 10:20, the divisions included:

- Many were saying He has a demon.
- Many were saying He is insane.
- Many were asking "Why do you listen to Him?"
- Others were saying these are not the sayings of one demon possessed.
- A demon cannot open the eyes of the blind, can he?

"The Jews gathered around Him, and were saying to Him, 'How long will You keep us in suspense? If you are the Christ (the Messiah, the Anointed One), tell us plainly."

(John 10:24)

Jesus answers them by bringing them back to the main problem: Belief.

> *"Jesus answered them, 'I told you, and* you do not believe; *the works that I do in my Father's name, these bear witness of Me. But* you do not believe *because you are not my sheep. My sheep hear my voice, and I know them, they follow Me; and I give eternal life to them, and they shall never perish; and no one shall snatch them out of My hand. My Father, Who has given them to Me, is greater than all; and no one is able to snatch them out of the Father's hand. I and the Father are one (a unity, one essence and person).'"*
> (John 10:25-30, emphasis and addition mine)

You've probably heard the old saying, "Sticks and stones may break my bones, but words can never harm me." Apparently, Jesus' words harmed them, and they tried to harm back with stones.

> *"Jesus answered them, 'I showed you many good works from the Father; for which of them are you stoning Me?'"*
> (John 10:32)

The Jews then identified what Jesus was trying to do.

> *"The Jews answered Him, 'For a good work we do not stone You, but* for the blasphemy; *and because You*, being a man, make Yourself out to be God.'"
> (John 10:33, emphasis mine)

The Jews did not believe that Jesus was God, the very thing

that John wrote about at the beginning of the Gospel of John.

> *"In the beginning was the Word and the Word was with God and the Word was God. He was in the beginning with God and the Word became flesh and dwelt among us and we beheld His glory as of the only begotten from the Father, full of grace and truth."*
> (John 1:1-2, John 1:14)

> *"If I do not do the works of my Father, do not believe in Me; but if I do them, though you do not believe Me, believe the works, that you may know and understand that the Father is in Me and I in the Father."*
> (John 10:37-38)

The-cause-and-effect of the words of Jesus caused the Pharisees to try to seize Jesus, but He eluded and escaped their actions.

> *"And* many believed *in Him there."*
> (John 10:42, emphasis mine)

WRITTEN THAT YOU MAY BELIEVE

Lord, I believe in the works, I believe in Your words, and Lord I believe in You and Your abundant life.

11

LAZARUS UNWRAPPERS

"He who had died came forth, bound hand and foot with wrappings and his face wrapped around with a cloth. Jesus said to them, 'Unbind/Unwrap him, and let him go."
(John 11:44, addition mine)

The name Lazarus has become synonymous with someone or something that has been raised from the dead. As you read through the story in John 11:1-42, we see that:

- A certain man was sick.
- The man was Lazarus of Bethany.
- Lazarus had two sisters named Mary and Martha.
- Mary was the lady who anointed the Lord with ointment and then wiped His feet with her hair.
- The sisters sent for Jesus identifying Lazarus as the one whom He (Jesus) loved.
- Jesus loved Martha, Mary, and Lazarus.

- Jesus did not go immediately to them but stayed two more day where He was.
- Jesus said to His disciples, "Let us go to Judea again."
- The disciples tried to reason with Jesus that the Jews were seeking to destroy Him.
- Jesus told them that if anyone walks in the day, he does not stumble, because he sees the light of this world, but in contrast, anyone walks in the night, he stumbles, because the light is not in him.
- Then Jesus told them that our friend Lazarus has fallen asleep.
- Jesus defines why they were going, that He may wake Lazarus from his sleep.
- The disciples reasoned if he has fallen asleep, then he will recover.
- Jesus plainly defined what He meant about Lazarus falling asleep: "Lazarus is dead."
- Jesus tells them why He was glad that He was not there at the time. The reason: "Lazarus is dead, and I am glad for your sakes that I was not there, *so* that you may believe; but let us go him."
- Thomas who was called Didymus spoke to the others and said for them to go and die with Him.

NOTE: He was speaking of Jesus being stoned by the Jews and they would die also.

- Lazarus had been in the tomb for four days.
- Martha went to meet with Jesus (Mary stayed home) and told Him that if He had been there, Lazarus would not have died.

- Martha told Jesus that even now, whatever He asks of God, God will give it to Him
- Jesus told her that God would raise Lazarus would rise again.
- Martha believed in the resurrection on the last day and told Jesus so.
- Jesus declared that not only would there be a resurrection, but that He was the *resurrection* and the *life* and he who *believes* in Him shall never die. He then asks the question of Martha, "*Do you believe this?*" (John 11:26, emphasis mine)
- Mary confessed, "Yes, Lord, *I have believed* that you are the Christ, the Son of God, even He Who comes into the world." (John 11:27, emphasis mine)

NOTE: Again, the idea of believing is being woven throughout the Gospel of John.

> *"Jesus said to him, 'Because you have seen Me, have you believed? Blessed are they who did not see, and yet believed. Many other signs therefore Jesus also performed in the presence of the disciples which are not written in this book, but these things have been written that you may believe that Jesus is the Christ, the Son of God; and that believing you may have life in His name."*
>
> (John 20:29-31)

- Apparently, Martha *believed*.

Jesus ordered the stone to be rolled away and Martha let Jesus know that, since Lazarus was dead for four days, that there would be a stench inside the tomb. I believe some versions of the Bible say it this way, "... he stinketh." Jesus reminded her that she needed to believe if she wanted to see the glory of God. In this case, the "glory of God" was resurrection from the dead.

As they removed the stone, Jesus prayed to the Father. He knew that the Father heard Him when He prayed, but He was praying that those around would hear and believe that He was sent by the Father. (John 11:4-42) Jesus then spoke three words,

"Lazarus, come forth."

(John 11:43)

Some biblical scholars believe that if Jesus had not identified the dead man by his name that every dead body would come forth.

The dead man, Lazarus came forth.

- He was bound hand and foot.
- He was bound with wrappings.
- His face was wrapped around with a cloth.

At this point Jesus spoke to those who had seen this miracle take place and told them to remove the wrappings, thus the title of this chapter: Lazarus Un-wrappers.

"...unbind him, and let him go."

(John 11:44)

Many years ago, I heard and Charles Thompson, an evangelist, preach a message called Lazarus Up-wrappers. He spoke about how Jesus sets people free but uses other people to deal with the things that continue to bind them. Surely Jesus could have called Lazarus forth and loosened the things still binding him. Again, we see that people believed because of His works.

> *"Many therefore of the Jews, who had come to Mary and beheld what and beheld what He had done, believed in Him."*
>
> (John 11:45, emphasis mine)

WRITTEN THAT YOU MAY BELIEVE

Lord, I believe that You are the Resurrection and the Life, and that because You were resurrected from the dead, so will I be.

12

DEATH OF A GRAIN

"Truly, truly, I say to you, unless a grain of wheat falls into the earth and dies, it remains by itself alone; but if it dies, it bears much fruit."

(John 12:24)

This verse about wheat falling to earth, dying, and bearing much fruit, is preceded by John 12:23, where Jesus states that His hour has come to be glorified. This glorification of Jesus will be the ultimate of bearing much fruit. His wheat moment was coming on the cross as He would hang on the cross and become the propitiation (satisfactory substitute) for our sins. Hanging on the cross, Jesus became a curse in our place so that we would not have to be cursed. (Galatians 3:13, Deuteronomy 31:23)

"Christ has redeemed us from the curse of the Law, having become a curse for us—for it is written, 'Cursed is everyone

who hangs on a tree,' in order that in Christ Jesus the blessing of Abraham might come to the Gentiles, so that we might receive the promise of the Spirit through faith."
(Galatians 3:13-14)

It has been said that a seed has everything within it to produce like kind. If you plant corn, you harvest corn in return; if you plant green beans, you harvest green beans in return; if you plant okra, you harvest okra in return. The diversity of harvest is as diverse as the seeds that you plant in the ground. One thing that they all have in common, from wheat to okra, is a seed that is planted in the ground. Before that seed produces, it must die. The seed comes under the trifecta of the pressure of the soil around it, the water, and the warmth, producing the death of the seed.

Once that seed dies, it cracks open. Roots descend as the plant begins its ascent to the surface, breaking through the soil, and reaching up towards the One who created the seed. It then goes through the process of growth, with the end result being harvest. The kingdom of God is compared to this planting and growth process.

> *"And He was saying, 'The kingdom of God is like a man who casts seed upon the soil; and he goes to bed at night and gets up by day, and the seed sprouts and grows—how, he himself does not know. The soil produces crops by itself; first the blade, then the head, then the mature grain in the head."*
> (Mark 4:26-28)

> *"And He said, 'So is the kingdom of God, as if a man should cast seed into the ground; and should sleep, and rise*

night and day, and the seed should spring and grow up, he knoweth not how.' And He said, 'So is the kingdom of God, as if a man should cast seed into the ground;'"

(Mark 4:26-28, KJV)

"And He said, 'The kingdom of God is like a man who scatters seed upon the ground, and then continues sleeping and rising night and day while the seed sprouts and grows and increases—he knows not how. The earth produces [acting] by itself—first the blade, then the ear, then the full grain in the ear. But when the grain is ripe and permits, immediately he sends forth [the reapers] and puts in the sickle, because the harvest stands ready.'"

(Mark 4:26-28, AMP)

The process includes:

- The seed cast upon the soil into the ground.
- The sower going to bed at night.
- Getting up next day.
- The seed sprouts (springs up) and grows.
- We do not understand how.
- First the blade appears.
- Then the head appears.
- Then the mature grain in its head.

"He who loves his life loses it; and he who hates his life in the world shall keep it to life eternal. If anyone serves Me, let him follow Me; and where I am, there shall My servant also be; if any one serves Me, the Father will honor me."

(John 12:25-26)

Jesus served at the pleasure of the Father in the Death, Burial, and Resurrection. As we die to ourselves daily (1 Corinthians 15:31) we live and are raised from the dead.

WRITTEN THAT YOU MAY BELIEVE

Lord, I believe that You died on the cross, were buried dead in a tomb, and on the third day, You rose from the dead. Lord, I believe that because of what You did, I became part of Your harvest.

13

THE EXAMPLE

"You call Me Teacher and Lord; and you are right; for so I am. If I then, the Lord and Teacher, washed your feet, you also ought to wash one another's feet for I gave you an example *that you also should do as I did to you."*

(John 13:15, emphasis mine)

I love the fact that God not only tells what we need to be doing, but He also gives us examples from the Old Testament (fat part of the book) and the New Testament (skinny part of the book).

"But God demonstrates (shows us how to do it) His own love toward us, in that while we were yet sinners, Christ died for us."

(Romans 5:8, addition mine)

NOTE: If we are going to follow the example and

demonstration of love, we will have to implement the yet factor and love before the sinners repent.

"Now these things happened as examples for us, so that we would not crave evil things as they also craved."
(1 Corinthians 10:6)

NOTE: The example given to us of Old Testament wilderness wanderers was to keep from happening to us what had happened to them; being "laid low in the wilderness."

"Now these things happened to them as an example, and they were written for our instruction, upon whom the ends of the age have come."
(1 Corinthians 10:11)

NOTE: It is so important for us to not be, "laid low in the wilderness," that God gives an example the second time.

Before the Feast of the Passover, Jesus knew things that did not keep Him from doing what He knew He had to do. It has been said that, if you keep your focus, you will accomplish your purpose in life. Jesus had focus and purpose.

"Therefore, since we have so great a cloud of witnesses surrounding us (see Hebrews 11:1-40 a.k.a. The Hall of Faith) let us also lay aside every encumbrance and the sin which so easily entangles/besets us and let us run with endurance the race that is set before us, fixing our eyes on Jesus, the author and perfecter (finisher) of faith (Jesus is our

example), Who for the joy set before Him endured the cross, despising the shame and has sat down at the right hand of the throne of God."

(Hebrews 12:1-2 addition mine)

"...the Son of God appeared for this purpose, that He might destroy the works of the d-evil."

(1 John 3:8, addition mine)

Jesus knew:

- His hour had come.
- He should depart out of this world to the Father.
- He loved His own who were in the world.
- He loved them to the end.

This supper was going to be a time of betrayal (by Judas), and a time of a teaching example, and a demonstration of humility.

We have already mentioned some things that Jesus knew, but now we see three more things He knew that would get Him through this final meal in John 13:3.

- Knowing that the Father had given all things into His hands (authority)
- Knowing that He had come forth from God (origin)
- Knowing that He was going back to the Father (destiny)

With this knowledge base, the Lord demonstrated a simple lesson in serving.

He did the unspeakable, which blew Peter's mind. (John 13:4-6)

NOTE: This act of a servanthood in John 13:4 reflects what took place in John 13:3

- Jesus *rose* from supper.
- Jesus *laid aside* His garments.
- Jesus *took* a towel.
- Jesus *girded* Himself about His waist.
- Jesus *poured* water into a basin.
- Jesus began to *wash* the disciples' feet.
- Jesus *wiped* them with the girded towel.

One by one, Jesus washed the disciples' feet. One can only imagine what Peter was thinking as Jesus came closer and closer to him. Once he moved the basin in front of Peter, we do not have to wonder any longer.

"And so He came to Simon Peter, He said to Him, 'Lord do you wash my feet?' Jesus answered and said to him, "What I do you do not realize now; but you shall understand hereafter."'
(John 13:6-7)

NOTE: Remember that Peter was watching the foot washing taking place from disciple to disciple, giving him plenty of time to formulate his response to Jesus.

"Peter said to Him, 'Never shall You wash my feet."
(John 13:8)

NOTE: Peter just said, "No," to Jesus.

"Jesus answered him, *'If I do not wash you, you have not part with Me.'*"

(John 13:8)

NOTE: Peter weighed his options to be part with Jesus or not be part with Jesus.

"*Simon Peter said to Him, 'Lord, not my feet only, but also my hands and my head.'*"

(John 13:9)

"*Jesus answered, 'He who has bathed needs only to wash his feet, but is completely clean; and you are clean, but not all of you (referring to Judas and his betrayal).*"

(John 13:10-11, addition mine)

Later on, we will see in John 15:1-3 Jesus speaking about fruit on the vine being taken away (lifted up and suspended and mud washed off the fruit) and then relating this to his disciples when He said,

"'*You are already clean because of the word which I have spoken to you.*'"

(John 15:3)

Jesus finished the foot washing and then returned to the table and asked them a question.

"'*Do you know what I have done to you?' Then He answered His own question. '"You call Me Teacher and*

Lord; and you are right; for so I am. If I then, the Lord and Teacher, washed your feet, you also ought to wash one another's feet, for I gave you and example that you also should do as I did for you."

(John 13:12-15, emphasis mine)

There it is; the reason for washing their feet was an example for them—and us—to be servants to one another and not to think more highly of themselves/ourselves or their/our rank in the kingdom.

WRITTEN THAT YOU MAY BELIEVE

Lord, I do believe what You demonstrated by washing Your disciples' feet. Lord. I believe that, if I want to be great in God's Kingdom, I must learn, "to be the servant of all." (Matthew 20:26)

14

ANOTHER HELPER/COMFORTER

"And I will ask the Father, and He will give you another Helper/Comforter, that He may be with you forever."
(John 14:16, emphasis and addition mine)

H ELPER/COMFORTER: paraklētos (par-ak'-lay-tos)-An intercessor, consoler:- advocate, comforter. (Strong's)

NOTE: Jesus was going to ask the Father to give, "another Helper/Comforter." It has been said by various teachers and scholars—including Rick Renner from "Sparkling Gems from The Greek" and W.E. Vine, Merrill F. Unger and William White, Jr. from "Vines Complete Expository Dictionary of Old Testament Words"—that the word "allos" for "another" means "one of the same kind," versus "homo" meaning "one of a different kind." If "allos" or "one of the same kind" is the meaning, it makes sense that the Holy Spirit is not Someone with a different agenda from Jesus. The same mission that Jesus, the Comforter, came to do would be continued through

His followers because the Helper would be like Jesus; it would not be a different purpose or agenda.

- Jesus had made an appearance on planet Earth 33-years earlier in the form of a baby (Luke 2:1-7).
- He grew in wisdom and stature (Luke 2:52).
- After He was obedient in baptism, He received the anointing of the Holy Spirit and power (Matthew 4:11-17).
- He was tempted in the wilderness (Matthew 4:1-11, Luke 4:1-13).
- He began a three-year ministry of doing good and healing all who were oppressed by the d-evil (Matthew 4:23-25, Acts 10:38).
- His purpose was to destroy the works of the d-evil (1 John 3:8) by the death, burial and resurrection on the cross (1 Corinthians 15:1-5).

Now Jesus was meeting with His disciples to give the farewell discourse. In John 14:1-17 we see:

- Jesus telling them not to let their hearts be troubled (because He was leaving).
- Jesus told them to believe in God, believe also in Me,
- Jesus told them that He was going to prepare a place for them in His Father's house where there many dwelling places.
- Jesus promised them that if He goes to prepare a place for them, He will return for them.
- Jesus told them that they know the way where He was going.

- Thomas questioned Jesus about their knowing the way.

NOTE: This is the famous statement about the roadmap to where Jesus was going.

> *"Jesus said to Him, 'I am the way, and the truth and the life; no none comes to the Father, but through Me. If you had known Me, you would have known My Father also; from now on you know Him, and have seen Him."*
> (John 14:6-7)

NOTE: Jesus is telling them that they knew the Father because they had known Him, since Jesus and the Father were the same being.

> *"In the beginning was the Word (Jesus) and the Word (Jesus) was with God and the Word (Jesus) was God."*
> (John 1:1, addition and emphasis mine)

Phillip joins in the conversation and requested that Jesus show them the Father and that, if Jesus did that, it would be enough for them (John 14:8).

NOTE: Jesus quizzes Phillip about his request.

> *"Jesus said to him, 'Have I been so long with you and yet you have not come to know Me, Philip? He who has seen Me has seen the Father; how do you say, "show us the Father?" Do you not believe that I am in the Father, and the Father is in Me?*
>
> *"The words that I say to you I do not speak on My own*

initiative, but the Father abiding in Me does His works."
(John 14:9-10)

The core of Jesus' response was for them to believe. In John 14:11-15, we see He wanted them to:

- Believe that He was in the Father.
- Believe that the Father was in Him.
- Or believe on account of the works (that they had seen for three years).
- If they believe in Jesus, the works that He did they would do also, and greater works would they do because He was going to the Father.
- Whatever they would ask (in reference to the greater works), they would do so the Father would be glorified in the works.
- If they ask anything (in reference to the works) in Jesus' name, Jesus said, "I will do it."
- Jesus said, "If you love Me, you will keep My commandments."

NOTE: John 14:21 speaks of disclosure from the Father that is hinged on love and obedience to His commandments.

"He who has My commandments and keeps them, he it is who loves Me; and he who loves Me shall be loved by My Father, and I will love him, and will disclose (reveal, manifest Myself to Him."
(John 14:21, addition mine)

NOTE: Walking in the greater works is based on having

the commandments (the Word of God), obedience to the commandments, loving the Father/Jesus, and The Holy Spirit (the Helper, the Comforter) that Jesus will be sending back when He leaves.

As has been said earlier, when Jesus states that He will be sending back another Helper/Comforter, the word for another is allos (one of the same kind). Yes, the Holy Spirit is the Helper/Comforter, but Jesus was the Comforter also. There is no change or shift in agenda when Jesus leaves; the mission continues with the Holy Spirit in the believers.

WRITTEN THAT YOU MAY BELIEVE

Lord, I believe that the Helper/Comforter will be with me as I walk in the greater works, and the fact is that You will be doing them through me.

15

THE CONNECTION

"I am the vine, you are the branches; he who abides in Me, and I in him, he bears much fruit; for apart from Me you can do nothing."

(John15:7)

There was a singer named Keith Green who put a spin on this verse by doing a play on the words de-vine and de-branches.

NOTE: I highly recommend a book by Bruce Wilkinson (author of "The Prayer of Jabez") called "The Secrets of the Vine." He goes into depth about Jesus' teaching on how to bear various levels of fruit and the process of caring for the vine.

The cast of characters in Jesus' teaching includes:

- Jesus: the true vine
- Jesus' Father: the vinedresser

- Jesus' disciples/us/you/me: the branches

Throughout His teaching, there is a connection between all three—the vine, the vinedresser, and the branches—resulting in various levels of fruit production. The branches will bear:

- Fruit
- More fruit
- Much fruit

The key to fruit production is taking the fruit out of the mud, cleansing the fruit and then suspending the fruit so it will not be lying on the ground which hinders fruit production. There is a pruning process, a cutting away dead wood that takes it to the next level, from bearing fruit to bearing more fruit. Then we see the concept of the branches abiding in the vine that bears much fruit.

ABIDE: menō (men'-o)=A primary verb; to stay (in a given place, state, relation or expectancy): - abide, continue, dwell, endure, be present, remain, stand, tarry (for), X thine own. (Strong's)

The idea is perseverance, not giving up. As believers, when there are trials, troubles and tribulations, sometimes, we tend to not abide or continue. In the gospels, in Jesus' parable of the sower/seed/soil, we see the various levels of soil representing the heart, which has the seed (the Word of God) planted, and there are attacks on the soil for the Word's/seed's sake.

SOIL SAMPLES

Jesus taught using parables that people could relate to and would drive the spiritual point home in their hearts. In this parable, found in Matthew, Mark, and Luke:

1. Seed: The seed is the Word of God
2. Soil: The soil is the heart of the hearer.
3. There are four soil samples/conditions:

- The soil beside the road. This soil has the Word sown in the heart and the bird (satan) came and takes away the word that has been sown.
- The soil of rocky soil. The person hears the Word and immediately receives it with joy. However, because they have no firm root in themselves, it is only temporary; when affliction or persecution arises because of the Word, they immediately fall away.
- The soil with thorns. The person also heard the Word, but the worries, deceitfulness of riches, and the desires for other things enter in and choke the Word and it becomes unfruitful
- The good soil. This person hears the Word, accepts it and bears fruit, thirty-, sixty-, and hundred-fold.

"And the seed in the good ground, these are the ones who have heard the word in an honest and good heart, and hold it fast, and bear fruit with perseverance."
(Luke 8:15, Mark 4:20, Matthew 5:15)

This is what it means to abide and not give up. Perseverance and keeping on keeping on, staying connected to the vine, will allow the branches to bear much fruit. This is not only good for fruit production but also for productive prayers.

> *"I (Jesus) am the vine, you (followers of Jesus) are the branches; he who abides (continues, dwells, takes up residence) in Me (the vine/Jesus), and I (Jesus/the vine) in him (us) bears much fruit, for* apart from Me you can do nothing.*"*
>
> (John 15:5, addition and emphasis mine)

NOTE: If I could just learn this one lesson; that apart from Jesus I can do nothing.

This abiding is also critical if you want answered prayers concerning the things of God. My problem is that when I pray, and I don't get immediate results, I give up. I try to do things apart from Jesus, which ends up with me not being able to do anything. When I abide, when I stay connected to the vine, and don't give up, things start to happen, and fruitfulness comes into my life.

> *"If you abide in Me, and My words abide in you, ask whatever you wish, and it shall be done for you."*
>
> (John 15:7)

WRITTEN THAT YOU MAY BELIEVE

Lord, I believe that I must stay connected with You, abide in You, and You in me if I ever want to bear fruit and have answered prayers.

16

DO YOU NOW BELIEVE

"Do you now believe?"

(John 16:31)

From John Chapter Fourteen until now, Jesus has been preparing His followers for His departure from planet Earth. In John 14:1-18, He has assured them that:

- He is preparing a house for them within His Father's house.
- They will follow Him there at some point.
- He and the Father are the same.
- They will do the same work that He has done for three years and even greater works.
- All of this is because He is going to the Father.
- When He gets there, He will send another comforter, one of the same kind as He is.
- He will not leave them as orphans.

The name and premise for this book is that it was, written that you may believe (John 20:31) We continue with that premise, as Jesus asked His disciples,

"Do you now believe?"

(John 16:31)

Jesus continues from Chapter Fourteen preparing His followers for His departure back to the Father. He had stated,

"A little while, and you will no longer behold Me; and again a little while and you will see Me."

(John 16:16)

They had been with Him for three years and now He is speaking in cryptic (but plain) words about going away. These types of statements sparked conversation between the disciples.

"Some of his disciples therefore said to one another, 'What is this thing He is telling us, "a little while, and you will not behold Me; and again a little while, and you will see Me" and "Because I go to the Father"'?

(John 16:17)

"And so they were saying, 'What is this that He says, "a little while?" We do not know what He is talking about.'"

(John 16:18)

When someone is talking to you and you do not know what they are talking about, it is hard to believe. The good news is that Jesus would further explain to His disciples what He was talking about and then He would ask them,

> *"Do you now believe?"*
> (John 16:31)

> *"Jesus knew that they wished to question Him…"*
> (John 16:18)

The good news for us is that Jesus knows what questions we have. The good news for us is that we can ask Him anything and He will take time and bring us to the point that we can believe.

> *"Jesus knew that they wished to question Him, and He said to them, 'Are you deliberating together about this, that I said, "A little while, and you will not behold Me, and again a little while, and you will see Me?"*
> (John 16:19)

Here are a few things that Jesus explained to them in John 16:20-30 to help them with their deliberation and bring them to the point of believing:

- You will weep and lament, but the world will rejoice.
- You will be sorrowful, but *your sorrow will be turned into joy.*
- When a woman is in travail she has sorrow, because her hour is come.
- When a woman gives birth to the child, she remembers

that anguish no more, for joy that a child has been born into the world.

NOTE: There will be momentary sorrow as Jesus departs back to the Father, but joy will come with His return.

- Therefore, [Always see what *therefore* is *there for* by reading the previous statement.
- You too, now have sorrow; but I will see you again, and your heart will rejoice, and no one takes your joy away from you.

NOTE: In Acts 1:9-11, Jesus had finished his B.I.B.L.E (Basic Instructions Before Leaving Earth) and He left Earth.

"And after He has said these things, He was lifted up while they were looking on, and a cloud received Him out of their sight. And as they were gazing intently into the sky while He was departing, behold, two men in white clothing stood beside them; and they also said, 'Men of Galilee, why do you stand looking into the sky? This Jesus, who has been taken up from you into heaven, will come in just the same way as you watched Him go into heaven.'"

(Acts 1:9-11)

In John 16:19-27, Jesus tells them:

- You will ask Me (Jesus) no question in that day.
- If you shall ask the Father for anything, He will give it to you in My name.
- Up until know you have asked for nothing in My name.

- Ask and you will receive, that your joy may be made full
- Jesus had been speaking to them in figurative language
- There will be a time that He will speak to them no more in figurative language, but will tell them plainly of the Father
- They will ask in Jesus' name and have access to the Father
- The Father Himself loves you because you have loved Jesus and you have *believed* that Jesus came forth from the Father.

Jesus now shifts from figurative language to plain language:

"I came forth from the Father and come into the world; I am leaving the world again and going to the Father."
(John 16:28)

Jesus is underscoring what He knew in John 13:

"Jesus knowing that the Father had given all things into His hands, and that He had come forth from God, and was going back to God."
(John 13:3)

At this point, His disciples saw that Jesus was speaking plainly, and that Jesus was not using figures of speech. The cause-and-effect was they entered into a new realm of believing. In John 16:30, they:

- Knew all things.
- Had no need for anyone to question Jesus.

- Stated, "We *believe that You came from God.*"

This was the answer from Jesus and He asks us the same thing: "Jesus answered them, 'Do you now believe?'"

WRITTEN THAT YOU MAY BELIEVE

Lord, I believe that You came from the Father, that You went back to the Father, and that You will be returning back for me.

17

TRUTH

"Sanctify them in truth; Thy word is truth."

(John 17:17)

In the Gospel of Matthew 6:6-15, and Luke 11:1-1-4, we have what is known as "The Lord's Prayer." Jesus' disciples had come and asked Him to teach them to pray like John the Baptist's disciples. Jesus did not rebuke them but taught them principles and concepts of praying.

THE LORD'S PRAYER (Matthew 6:9-15)

Before Jesus gave them the outline for prayer, He underscored the fact that, even before they prayed, the Father already knew what they needed. Our prayer is a collaborative effort between the one praying and the One answering the prayer.

- *Our Father: Not only is God Jesus' Father, but He is also our Father.*

- *Who art in Heaven: Jesus, God in the flesh was on planet Earth, but the One who answers our prayers is in Heaven.*

- *Hallowed be Thy Name: "Hallowed" means to make holy, purify, to consecrate His name which we know is already holy. When we hallow His name, we are not making it something that it already is, we are merely making it so in our personal lives.*

- *Your kingdom come: We are asking for His rule and reign and foundation of power to come into our lives and our world.*

- *Your will be done: We are asking for His wish and desire to be accomplished in our lives.*

- *On Earth: The place where we live and where sickness and sin is rampant and where the d-evil is the god (little g) of this world.*

- *As it is in Heaven: Where there is no sickness and sin but only healing and holiness is. We want His will as it is in Heaven not as it is on Earth.*

- *Gives us this day our daily bread: This speaks of our total reliance, each and every day, on His presence and provision.*

- *And forgive us our debts/trespasses as we also have forgiven our debtors/trespassers: Without Jesus, we*

- *owe a debt. There is a song from the seventies, about the fact that I owed a debt that I could never pay and the fact the Jesus paid that debt. The cause-and-effect was that I could then sing a brand-new song about the Amazing Grace given me.*

- *And do not lead us into temptation: To be tempted is to be enticed away from the purposes of God. Instead of temptation, we are to pray to be delivered from evil.*

- *For Yours is the kingdom (where the King rules), and the power (authority and dynamic ability) and the glory (the shining of His presence) forever (and that is a long time). Amen. (So be it)*

Jesus continues His teaching:

- *For if you forgive others for their transgressions, your heavenly Father will also forgive you. But if you do not forgive others, then your Father will not forgive you your transgressions: If we want effective prayers, whatever we receive from the Father, we must give to others who do not deserve what we freely received.*

While Jesus taught them the method of prayer, it was not necessarily His prayer. Oh, Jesus prayed for sure. The Lord's Prayer is a wonderful model about how we should pray. But realize that Jesus was Someone Who prayed many times, in many places, in many manners. Jesus was a man of prayer.

"In the days of His flesh, when He offered up both

prayers and supplications *with loud crying and tears to Him who was able to save Him from death, and Who was heard because of His piety."*

(Hebrews 5:7, emphasis mine)

"And in the early morning, *while it was still dark, He arose and went out and* departed to a lonely place, *and* was praying there."

(Mark 1:35, emphasis mine)

"At that time Jesus answered and said, 'I praise Thee, O Father, Lord of heaven and earth *that Thou didst hide these things from the wise and intelligent and didst reveal them to babes. Yes, Father for thus it was well pleasing in Thy sight."*

(Matthew 11:25-26, emphasis mine)

"And after He had sent the multitudes away, He went up to the mountain by Himself to pray; *and when it was evening, He was there alone."*

(Matthew 14:23, emphasis mine)

"And it was at this time that He went off to the mountain to pray, *and* He spent the whole night in prayer to God."

(Luke 6:12, emphasis mine)

"*Simon, Simon, behold satan has demanded permission to sift you like wheat;* but I have prayed for you, *that your faith may not fail and you, when once you have turned again, strengthen your brothers."*

(Luke 22:31-32, emphasis mine)

"And He withdrew from them about a stone's throw, and He knelt down and began to pray, *saying, 'Father, if Thou art willing, remove this cup from Me; yet not My will but Thine be done.' Now an angel from heaven appeared to Him, strengthening Him. And being in agony He was praying* He was praying very fervently; *and His sweat became like drops of blood falling down upon the ground."*
(Luke 22:41-44, emphasis mine)

"But Jesus was saying, 'Father forgive them; *for they do not know what they are doing,' and they cast lots, dividing up His garments among themselves."*
(Luke 23:34, emphasis)

"And so they removed the stone (from Lazarus' tomb). And Jesus raised His eyes, and said, 'Father, I thank Thee that Thou heardest Me. *And I knew that* Thou hearest Me *always but because of the people standing around I did it,* that they may believe *that Thou didst send Me.'"*
(John 11:41-42, addition and emphasis mine)

"Now my soul has become troubled; *and what* shall I say *Father, save Me from this hour? But for this purpose I came to this hour. Father, glorify Thy name. There came therefor a voice out of heaven: 'I have both glorified it, and will glorify it again.'"*
(John 12:27-28, emphasis mine)

Jesus was well acquainted with prayer. In John 17, we see Jesus praying again. Some say—and I agree—that the prayer in John 17 is the real Lord's Prayer.

> "*These things* Jesus spoke; and lifting up His eyes to heaven *He said, 'Father, the hour has come; glorify Thy Son, that the Son may glorify Thee, even as Thou gavest Him authority over all mankind, that to all whom Thou has given Him, He may give eternal life.'"*
>
> (John 17:1-2, emphasis mine)

The whole chapter is rich with the conversation between Jesus and the Father; but for our purpose, we will glean a few things later on in the prayer. Here is a breakdown of Jesus's request for His followers found in John 17:17-23:

- Sanctify them in the truth; Thy Word is truth.
- As Thou didst send Me into the world, I also have sent them into the world.
- For their sakes, I sanctify Myself, that they themselves also may be sanctified in the truth.
- I do not ask in behalf of these alone, but those also who believe in Me through their words.

NOTE: We are the ones that Jesus prayed for who would believe in Him through the disciples' words. The disciples made disciples and taught those disciples all the words that Jesus had taught them. They passed on those words throughout generations, up to you and me.

- That they may all be one; even as Thou, Father art in Me and I in Thee, that they also may be in Us; that the world may believe that Thou didst send Me.
- The glory which Thou has given Me I have given them; that thy may be one, just as We are One.

- I in them, Thou in Me, that they may be perfected in unity, that the world may know that Thou didst send Me and didst love them, even as Thou didst love Me.

Wow, now that is a prayer. The old Jewish say was, "From your lips to God's ear." I believe that Jesus' prayer was heard by the Father and the Father will answer that prayer back then and now.

WRITTEN THAT YOU MAY BELIEVE

Lord, I believe that Your Words are truth and that I will be and am being sanctified in truth.

18

WHAT IS TRUTH

"Pilate said to Him, "What is truth?"
(John 18:38)

In the previous chapter, we see that truth is defined as the sanctifying agent.
"Sanctify them in the truth; Thy word is truth."
(John 17:17)

SANCTIFY: hagiazō (hag-ee-ad'-zo)=From G40; to make holy, that is, (ceremonially) purify or consecrate; (mentally) to venerate: - hallow, be holy, sanctify. G40: hagios (hag'-ee-os-)=From hagos (an awful thing), sacred (physically pure, morally blameless or religious, ceremonially consecrated): - (most) holy (one, thing), saint. (Strong's)

GODISNOWHERE

When I was recently in the hospital with a stroke, there were at least twelve days where I was awake, alert, responsive, following commands; but I do not remember anything I said or did. One thing that I did (without knowing what I was doing) was had someone write on the board in my room in ICU (intensive care unit) "GODISNOWHERE." Actually, while in ICU, I first had Brenda write on a piece of paper the phrase; once I transferred to a regular room I had them write it on a dry erase board.

Apparently, whenever someone came in the room—nurse, tech, neurologist, primary physician—I would ask them to read the message on the board said.

Some would say, "God is nowhere." I would then ask them to read it again. Then they would see it and say, "God is now here." It really depends on how you look at it and how you perceive it. In each incident. the person reading would think and believe that they were reading the truth until they saw the real truth.

How you perceive the truth will determine how you will act in this world. You can believe a lie and act on a lie, but it will never be the truth.

In previous chapters, we have seen Jesus filling His followers in on about what was about to happen to Him. Now we are smack dab in the middle of the beginning of what is known as His Passion. Jesus had been betrayed by Judas; defended by Peter as he cut off the year of Malchus, the servant of the high priest; arrested by soldiers, and then denied by Peter. Jesus was then brought before Pontius Pilate. (John 18:1-27)

The Christian rock group, Petra (*petra* is the Greek word for "massive rock") recorded a song, "Judas' Kiss." The song begins with backward masking which sounds like nonsensical sounds. If you play it backwards, it questions the listener why they are spinning the record backwards in attempts to look for a hidden message from the devil. What the listener ought to be doing is looking for the Lord. It then rocks into the question about wondering how it makes Jesus feel when the prodigal runs away. The bottom line is that it must make Jesus feel just as He felt when Judas betrayed Him with a kiss.

After questioning Jesus himself, the High Priest Caiaphas sent Jesus to Pilate. "Pontius Pilate was the fifth prefect of the Roman province of Judaea from AD 26–36. He served under Emperor Tiberius, and is best known today for the trial and crucifixion of Jesus." (Wikipedia) Caiaphas would not enter the Praetorium (governor's official residence) because he would be defiled and would not be able to eat the Passover. Pilate went out to the Jewish leaders and questioned them about the accusations brought against Jesus. They told Pilate that if He were not an evil doer, they would not have brought Him to Pilate. (John 18:28-30) Pilate attempted to give Jesus back to the Jewish leaders, but the crux of the matter was revealed.

> "...*the Jews said to him, 'We are not permitted to put anyone to death.'*"
>
> (John 18:31)

The religious leaders did not want to dirty their hands with the blood of an innocent man.

This would play into the hands of Jesus, because He had spoken...

"signifying by what kind of death He was about to die."
(John 18:32)

Pilate then began to question Jesus in John 18:33-38:

- Pilate entered the Praetorium.
- Jesus summoned Jesus.
- Pilate asked Jesus if He was the King of the Jews.
- Jesus asked Pilate if he had come up with this on his own initiative or had others told Pilate about Him.
- Pilate declared that He was not a Jew.
- Pilate told Jesus that His own nation and chief priests had delivered Him up to him.
- Pilate asked Jesus what He had done.

At this point, Jesus began to explain the concept of His Kingdom versus the kingdom of the world.

- Jesus told Pilate that His kingdom is not of this world.
- Jesus told Pilate that, if His kingdom were of this world, then His servants would be fighting, that He might be delivered up to the Jews.
- Jesus underscores that His kingdom is not of this realm.
- Pilate picks up on the truth that Jesus is a King.

"...You say correctly that I am a king. For this I have been born, and for this I have come into the world, to bear witness to the truth. Everyone who is of the truth hears My voice."
(John 18:37)

Now comes to question from Pilate that Jesus has been defining for years.

> *"Pilate said to Him,* What is truth?*"*
> (John 18:38, emphasis mine)

> *"Jesus therefore was saying to those* Jews who had believed Him, *'If you abide in My word, then you are truly disciples of Mine; and y*ou shall know the truth, and the truth shall make you free."
> (John 8:31-32, emphasis mine)

> *"If therefore* the Son shall make you free, you shall be free indeed."
> (John 8:36, emphasis mine)

> *"Jesus said to him,* 'I am the way, and the truth, and the life; *no one comes to the Father but through Me.'"*
> (John 14:6, emphasis mine)

WRITTEN THAT YOU MAY BELIEVE

Lord, I believe that You are the Word in the beginning with God. I believe you are the Word and are God. I believe that You are the way, the truth and the life and You are the only way to the Father. I believe that your Word is truth.

19

GIVEN AUTHORITY

"Pilate therefore said to Him, 'You do not speak to me? Do You not know that I have authority to release, You, and I have authority to crucify You?' Jesus answered, 'You would have no authority over Me, unless it had been given you from above; for this reason he who delivered Me up to you has the greater sin.'"

(John 19:10-11)

AUTHORITY/POWER: exousia (ex-oo-see'-ah)=- From G1832 (in the sense of ability); privilege, that is, (subjectively) force, capacity, competency, freedom, or (objectively) mastery (concretely magistrate, superhuman, potentate, token of control), delegated influence: - authority, jurisdiction, liberty, power, right, strength. G1832: exesti (ex'-es-tee)=it is right (through the figurative idea of being out in public): - be lawful, let, X may (-est). (Strong's)

POWER: Dunamis (doo'-nam-is)=From G1410; force

(literally or figuratively); specifically miraculous power (usually by implication a miracle itself): - ability, abundance, meaning, might (-ily, -y, -y deed), (worker of) miracle (-s), power, strength, violence, mighty (wonderful) work. G1410: dunamai (doo'-nam-ahee)=Of uncertain affinity; to be able or possible: - be able, can (do, + -not), could, may, might, be possible, be of power. (Strong's)

This thing called power is a two-sided coin, with each side being a picture of what Jesus walked in on earth as He manifested the kingdom and the will of God on earth as it is in heaven. (Matthew 6:9)

Authority (exousia) comes from a higher power down to a lower power that gives the lower power the right to carry out the legal obligations required. On earth, the police have authority and carry a badge that represents that authority. The dunamis power is the dynamic ability to carry out what the exousia gives them the right to do. Jesus had the exousia authority from the Father to handle the oppression by the d-evil with dynamic dunamis ability.

> *"Thy Kingdom (rule and reign) come (be manifested), Thy will (wish, desire) be done (accomplished) on earth (where there is sickness and sin)* as it is *(just like it is) in heaven (where there is no sickness and sin)."*
> (Matthew 6:9, addition and emphasis mine)

Jesus knew a thing or two about authority and power. He exercised it for three years as He went about doing good and healing all who were oppressed by the d-evil for God was with Him. (Acts 10:38)

"And Jesus came up and spoke to them, saying 'All authority (exousia) has been given to Me in heaven and on earth.'"
(Matthew 28:18, addition mine)

"You know of Jesus of Nazareth, how God anointed Him with the Holy Ghost and with power (dunamis) and how He went about doing good and healing all who were oppressed by the d-evil for God was with Him."
(Acts 10:38, addition mine)

This anointing from God was yoke breaking, burden lifting, oppression removing, healing power of the Holy Ghost. NOTE: Say that a few times and see if it doesn't get you charged up.

Pilate thought he knew about power and authority. He could reason about things on an earthly level, but now he was encountering power and authority from another realm. The Kingdom of God extends from heaven to earth.

"The Kingdom of God is not meat or drink, but righteousness, peace and joy in the Holy Ghost."
(Romans 14:17)

KINGDOM: basileia (bas-il-i'-ah)=From G935; properly royalty, that is, (abstractly) rule, or (concretely) a realm (literally or figuratively): - kingdom, + reign. G935: basileus (bas-il-yooce')=Probably from G939 (through the notion of a foundation of power); a sovereign (abstractly, relatively or figuratively): - king. G939: basis (bas'-ece)=From bainō (to walk); a pace (base), that is, (by implication) the foot: - foot. (Strong's)

- Royalty
- Rule
- Realm
- Reign
- Foundation of power
- Sovereign
- King
- To walk
- A pace
- Base
- Foot

Earthly authority is merely a shadow of the real deal found from up above.

When Pilate tossed in the authority card, with power to crucify Jesus, Jesus pulled out the trump card about where Pilate's authority emanated from. His above authority trumped Pilate's earthly authority. Pilate realized he was the low authority on the totem pole. The cause-and-effect of this realization of the hierarchy of authority was to do the right thing.

> "As a result of this Pilate made efforts (was seeking to) release Him…"
>
> (John 19:12, addition mine)

WRITTEN THAT YOU MAY BELIEVE

Lord, I believe that all authority (legal right) and power (dynamic ability) comes from the Father, to You, to us, and I yield to the authority that comes from above.

20

LIFE IN HIS NAME

"Therefore many other signs Jesus also performed in the presence of the disciples, which are not written in this book; but these things ae written that you may believe that Jesus is the Christ, the Son of God; and that believing you may have life in His name."

(John 20:30-31, emphasis mine)

It is from Chapter Twenty of the Gospel of John that we get the premise for this book. In verses 30-31, there is listed a three-fold purpose for the writing of the gospel:

- That you may *believe* that *Jesus is the Christ.*
- That you may *believe* that *Jesus is the Son of God.*
- That you may *believe* and *have life in His name.*

As we have gone through the previous nineteen chapters, we have seen that there many more things to believe than these three reasons, but they all point to this trifecta for believing.

BELIEVE THAT JESUS IS THE CHRIST

CHRIST: Christos (khris-tos')=From G5548; anointed, that is, the Messiah, an epithet of Jesus: - Christ. G5548: chriō (khree'-o)=Probably akin to G5530 through the idea of contact; to smear or rub with oil, that is, (by implication) to consecrate to an office or religious service: - anoint. (Strong's)

> *"The Son of God appeared for this purpose, that He might destroy the works of the d-evil."*
> (1 John 3:8, addition mine)

> *"You know of Jesus of Nazareth how God anointed Him with the Holy Spirit and with power, and how He went about doing good, and healing all who were oppressed by the d-evil; for God was with Him."*
> (Acts 10:38, addition mine)

> *"And it shall come to pass in that day, that his burden shall be taken away from off thy shoulder, and his yoke from off thy neck, and the yoke shall be destroyed because of the anointing."*
> (Isaiah 10:27)

> *"And the book of the prophet Isaiah was handed to Him, and He opened the book and found the place where it was written, 'The Spirit of the Lord is upon Me, because He anointed Me to preach the gospel to the poor. He has sent Me*

to proclaim release to the captives, and recovery of sight to the blind, to set free those who are downtrodden, to proclaim the favorable year of the Lord.' And He closed the book, and gave it back to the attendant, and sat down; and the eyes of all in the synagogue were fixed upon Him. And He began to say to them, 'Today this Scripture has been fulfilled in your hearing.'"

(Luke 4:17-21)

When Jesus was in the district of Caesarea Philippi, in Matthew 16:13, He asked His disciples who the people were saying that He was. Their answers included a broad spectrum:

- John the Baptist
- Elijah
- Jeremiah
- One of the prophets

Jesus then asks the question that resonates to every person throughout history, from then until now.

"He said to them, 'But who do you say that I am?'"

(Matthew 16:15)

Simon Peter gave the correct answer.

- You are the Christ
- You are the Son of the living God.
- In essence, Peter said, "You are the Anointed One; the Messiah; the One who had contact with God; the One Who smeared on and rubbed into the oil of the

Holy Ghost; consecrated; sanctified; set apart for the purposes of God to destroy the works of the d-evil."

I believe that whenever you see the word, "Christ" you can think of more than just a title of a man. You can think of an anointing for yoke breaking, burden lifting, oppression removing power of the Holy Ghost. For example:

"Therefore, if any man is in Christ (the anointing of yoke breaking, burden lifting, oppression, removing, healing power of the Holy Ghost) he is a new creation, the old things passed away, behold new things are constantly coming."
(2 Corinthians 5:17, addition mine)

When you think about the power of the Anointed One and His anointing from God, it just makes sense that it is the anointing that can change a person.

When Peter gave the answer about Jesus being the Christ, the Anointed One, Jesus said,

"And Jesus said to him, 'Blessed are you, Simon Barjonah, because flesh and blood did not reveal this to you, but My Father Who is in heaven."
(Matthew 16:17)

Peter did not learn this information from Jerusalem Tech, but heavenly revelation directly from the Father, the One who anointed Jesus as The Anointed One, the Christ, The Messiah. Jesus then went on the tell Peter that he was Petros (Greek for little stone) and upon the petros—the massive rock, the rock of revelation that Jesus is the Christ, the living

Son of God—the church would be built. (Matthew 16:18)

BELIEVE THAT JESUS IS THE SON OF GOD

SON: Uihos (hwee-os')=Apparently a primary word; a "son" (sometimes of animals), used very widely of immediate, remote or figurative kinship: - child, foal, son. (Strong's)

GOD: theos (theh'-os)=Of uncertain affinity; a deity, especially (with G3588) the supreme Divinity; figuratively a magistrate; by Hebraism very: - X exceeding, God, god [-ly, -ward]. (Strong's)

> *"For God so loved the world that He gave His* only begotten Son, *that whosoever* believes *in Him shall not perish but have everlasting life."*
> (John 3:16, emphasis mine)

> *"He who has my commandments and keeps them, he it is who loves Me shall be loved by* My Father, *and I will love him, and will disclose (manifest, reveal) Myself to Him."*
> (John 14:21, addition and emphasis mine)

> *"He who believes in Him is not judged; he who does not believe has been judged already, because he has not believed in the* name of the only begotten Son of God.*"*
> (John 3:18, emphasis mine)

Throughout the Gospels, Jesus repeatedly rubbed the religious leaders the wrong way because He plainly stated that He was more than just someone from Israel. He was also more than just someone Who had temporary powers. He was not only linked to God by being His only begotten Son, but He was actually God in the flesh.

> *"In the beginning was the Word (Jesus) and the Word (Jesus) was with God) and the Word (Jesus) was God.*
> (John 1:1, addition mine)

One of the earmarks of the Anti-Christ (anti-yoke breaking, burden lifting, oppression removing, healing of the Holy Ghost) is denial that Jesus came (from heaven to earth) in the flesh (the form of a human being).

> *"Beloved, do not believe every spirit, but test the spirits to see whether they are from God, because many false prophets have gone out into the world. By this you know the Spirit of God; every spirit that confesses that Jesus Christ has come in the flesh is from God; and every spirit that does not confess Jesus (has come in the flesh) is not from God; that is the spirit of the anti-Christ of which you have hear that it is coming and not is already in the world."*
> (1 John 4:1-3, addition mine)

BELIEVE THAT YOU HAVE LIFE IN HIS NAME

LIFE: zōē (dzo-ay')=From G2198; life (literally or figuratively): - life (-time). G2198: zaō (dzah'-o)=A primary verb; to live (literally or figuratively): - life (-time), (a-) live (-ly), quick.

NAME: Onoma (on'-om-ah)= name" (literally or figuratively),

(authority, character): - called, (+ sur-) name (-d). (Strong's)

"And she will bear a Son; and you shall call His name Jesus, for it is He who will save His people from their sins.' Now all this took place that what was spoken by the Lord through the prophet might be fulfilled saying, 'Behold the virgin shall be with child and shall bear a Son and they shall call His name Immanuel, which translated means God with us.' And Joseph arose from his sleep and did as the angel of the Lord commanded him, and took her as his wife and kept her a virgin until she gave birth to a Son and he called His name Jesus."

(Matthew 1:21-23)

"The thief comes only to steal and kill and destroy; I came that they may have life, and have it abundantly."

(John 10:10)

"These things I have written to you who believe in the name of the Son of God, so that you may know that you have eternal life."

(1 John 5:13)

"And if we know that He hears us in whatever we ask, we know that we have the requests which we have asked from Him."

(1 John 5:15)

There is salvation in His name.

"She will bear a Son; and you shall call His name Jesus,

for He will save *His people from their sins."*
(Matthew 1:21, emphasis mine)

SAVE: sōzō (sode'-zo)=From a primary word (contraction for the obsolete saos, safe); to save, that is, deliver or protect (literally or figuratively): - heal, preserve, save (self), do well, be (make) whole. (Strong's)

In the name of Jesus, He will:

- Save
- Deliver
- Protect
- Heal
- Preserve
- Do well
- Make whole

WRITTEN THAT YOU MAY BELIEVE

Lord, I believe that You are the Christ anointed with yoke breaking, burden lifting oppression removing healing power of the Holy Ghost. I believe that You are the only begotten Son of God, born of the Father's will, and I believe that You came that I could have life and have an abundant life.

21

FOLLOW ME

"*...And when He had spoken this He said to him,* follow Me."

(John 21:19, emphasis mine)

"*...If I want him to remain until I come, what is that to you? You* follow Me!"

(John 21:22, emphasis mine)

"Follow me *and I will make you fishers of men."*
(Matthew 4:19, Mark 1:7, emphasis mine)

It's interesting that when Jesus first encountered His future followers, He told them to,

"Follow Me"

(Matthew 4:19, Mark 1:7)

and at the end of His life, the same command was given,

"You follow Me."

(John 21:19, John 21:22)

Jesus had appeared thirty-three years earlier in Bethlehem as a little baby boy born to the virgin Mary, with Joseph, a human father who had not contributed to the conception. For three years, Jesus ministered under the anointing of the Holy Spirit. He gathered around Him a band of men and told them to "Follow Me."

At the end of the three years, Jesus was crucified, buried, and then resurrected. He met with the true believers, fellowshipped with them, ate with them, and gave them final instructions.

It was at this last meeting that Jesus had an encounter with the disciple who had denied Him three times: Peter. This was the third time after His resurrection that Jesus was manifested to his disciples. (John 21:14)

"So when they had finished breakfast, Jesus said to Simon Peter..."

(John 21:15)

This is the conversation and encounter that Jesus had with Peter in John 21:15-22:

- Jesus said to Simon Son of John, "Do you love me more than these?"
- Peter responded, "Yes, Lord; you know that I love You."
- Jesus told him, "Tend My lambs."
- Jesus asked Peter a second time, "Simon son of John, do you love Me?"

- Peter answered a second time, "Yes, Lord; you know that I love You."
- Jesus told him, "Shepherd My sheep."
- Jesus asked Peter a third time, "Simon, son of John, do you love Me?"
- This time Peter was grieved because He asked him the same question a third time.
- Peter told Jesus, "Lord, You know all things; You know that I love You."
- Jesus told him, "Tend My sheep."

Depending on the version of the Bible that you choose to read, Peter was told to feed My sheep, tend My lambs, and shepherd My sheep.

Many people have tried to read some kind of cryptic message into Jesus' words. I believe He was getting the point across that He was leaving and that His followers needed to be taken care of while He will be gone. Jesus shifts the topic to what Peter will face in the future. (John 21:18-19)

- Jesus told Peter that when he was younger he used to gird himself and walked wherever He wished.
- Jesus then told him that when he grew older, he will stretch out his hands and someone else will gird him and bring him where he did not wish to go.
- Jesus had just signified by what kind of death Peter would glorify God.
- When Jesus had spoken these insights, He told Peter to do what He had told him when He first met him: "Follow Me."

Now it was time for Peter to shift the topic. (John 21:20-21)

- Peter turned around and saw the disciple whom Jesus loved. It was the one who had leaned back on His breast at the supper.
- Peter asked, "Lord who is the one who betrays You," and then asked Lord, "What about this man?"
- Jesus response was, "If I want him to remain until I come, what is that to you?"
- Jesus ends the conversation, again saying what He first spoke to Peter on the shores of the Sea of Galilee: *"You, follow Me."*

As we come to the end of our journey of belief, we see in John 21:24-25:

- The writer who was testifying to these things and who wrote these things is John.
- John knows that his testimony is true.
- There are also many other things which Jesus did.
- If the other things that Jesus did were written in detail, even the world itself could not contain the books that would be written.

> *"Therefore many other signs Jesus also performed in the presence of the disciples, which are not written in this book; but these have been written that you may believe that Jesus is the Christ, the Son of God; and that believing you may have life in His name."*
>
> (John 20:30-31)

WRITTEN THAT YOU MAY BELIEVE

Lord, I believe that I will continue to Follow You. I believe that I will feed Your sheep and tend to my own business.

22

WRITTEN THAT YOU MAY BELIEVE OVERVIEW

We have been on a journey through twenty-one chapters in the Gospel of John. In each chapter, we have gleaned reasons to believe (trust in, cling to, rely upon) our God.

I don't know about you, but as I have read this gospel, my faith in the faithfulness of God has increased. As I have read this book, I began to reflect on the revealed words and deeds of Jesus. My faith deepened, and I began to trust in, clung to, and rely upon the Lord more than when I started.

I wanted to review from each chapter the things that we have seen and have come to believe.

Chapter 1: Lord, I believe that You are the Word that became (God in the) flesh and dwelt among us.
Chapter 2: Lord, I believe that, like the wine that was the best for now, You are the best for me now.
Chapter 3: Lord, I believe that I can see and enter the Kingdom of God as I am born again, anew, from above.

Chapter 4: Lord, I believe that Your Holy Spirit within my human spirit gives me the opportunity to worship You in the truth of the Word of God.

Chapter 5: Lord, I believe that You can do both, to heal my sicknesses and to forgive me my sins.

Chapter 6: Lord, I believe that manna was temporary, but You are forever; and if You are forever, then I will live forever.

Chapter 7: Lord, I believe that with You dwelling in me, that as rivers flow out of You, they will flow out of me.

Chapter 8: Lord, I believe You, I believe Your Words, I believe Your truth and I believe that when You set me free, I will be free indeed (without a doubt)."

Chapter 9: Lord, I also believe, and I worship You as You have dealt with my sins. I believe that Your grace is truly amazing.

Chapter 10: Lord, I believe in the works, I believe in Your words and Lord I believe in You and Your abundant life.

Chapter 11: Lord, I believe that You are the resurrection and the life, and that because You were resurrected from the dead, so will I be.

Chapter 12: Lord, I believe that You died on the cross, was buried dead in a tomb, and on the third day You rose from the dead. Lord, I believe that because of what You did, I became part of your harvest.

Chapter 13: Lord, I do believe what You demonstrated by washing Your disciples' feet. Lord, I believe that if I want to be great in God's Kingdom, I must learn "to be the servant of all." (Matthew 20:26)

Chapter 14: Lord, I believe that the Helper/Comforter will be with me as I walk in the greater works, and the fact is You will be doing them through me.

Chapter 15: Lord, I believe that I must stay connected with You, abide in You, and You in me if I ever want to bear fruit and have answered prayers.

Chapter 16: Lord, I believe that You came from the Father, that You went back to the Father, and that You will be returning for me.

Chapter 17: Lord, I believe that Your Words are truth and that I will be, and am being, sanctified in truth.

Chapter 18: Lord, I believe that You are the Word in the beginning with God. I believe You are the Word and are God. I believe that You are the way, the truth and the life and are the only way to the Father. I believe that Your Word is truth.

Chapter 19: Lord, I believe that all authority (legal right) and power (dynamic ability) comes from the Father, to You, to us and I yield to the authority that comes from above.

Chapter 20: Lord, I believe that You are the Christ, anointed with yoke breaking, burden lifting oppression removing, healing power of the Holy Ghost. I believe that You are the only begotten Son of God, born of the Father's will. I believe that because You came, I can have life and have an abundant life.

Chapter 21: Lord, I believe that I will continue to Follow You. I believe that I will feed Your sheep and tend to my own business.

ABOUT THE AUTHOR

Rodney Boyd is a follower of Jesus Christ, husband, dad, Speech-Language Pathologist and 2nd degree Black Belt in Wado Ryu Karate. He has a passion for music of all styles, writing, teaching the Word of God and the martial arts.

He has been married to his high school sweetheart, Brenda for more than 40 years and together they have one son, Phillip, and a daughter-in-law, Jamie. Boyd bases his life on Colossians 3:17:

> "And whatever you do in word or deed, do all in the name of the Lord Jesus, giving thanks through Him to God the Father."

Also Available From

Rodney Boyd

Never Run a Dead Data
Pro-Verb Ponderings
Speaking and Hearing the Word of God
Chewing the Daily Cud, Vols 1-4

Also Available From

WordCrafts Press

Pressing Foward
   by April Poynter

Morning Mist: *Stories from the Water's Edge*
   by Barbie Loflin

Youth Ministry is Easy! *and 9 other lies*
   by Aaron Shaver

Chronicles of a Believer
   by Don McCain

Illuminations
   by Paula K. Parker & Tracy Sugg

A Scarlet Cord of Hope
   by Sheryl Griffin

www.wordcrafts.net

www.ingramcontent.com/pod-product-compliance
Lightning Source LLC
Chambersburg PA
CBHW021152080526
44588CB00008B/309